Big Sid's Vincati

Inspired by Sid Biberman's Vincent, a young artist made this sketch during a drag meet back in the late 1950s. Ever since, this logo has served as the calling card of Big Sid, a master mechanic whose work has earned him the love and respect of motorcyclists the world over.

Big Sid's Vincati

The Story of a Father, a Son, and the Motorcycle of a Lifetime

Matthew Biberman

HUDSON
STREET
PRESS

HUDSON STREET PRESS
Published by the Penguin Group
Penguin Group (USA) Inc., 375 Hudson Street, New York, New York 10014, U.S.A. •
Penguin Group (Canada), 90 Eglinton Avenue East, Suite 700, Toronto, Ontario, Canada
M4P 2Y3 (a division of Pearson Penguin Canada Inc.) • Penguin Books Ltd., 80 Strand,
London WC2R 0RL, England • Penguin Ireland, 25 St. Stephen's Green, Dublin 2, Ireland
(a division of Penguin Books Ltd.) • Penguin Group (Australia), 250 Camberwell Road,
Camberwell, Victoria 3124, Australia (a division of Pearson Australia Group Pty. Ltd.) •
Penguin Books India Pvt. Ltd., 11 Community Centre, Panchsheel Park, New Delhi –
110 017, India • Penguin Group (NZ), 67 Apollo Drive, Rosedale, North Shore 0632,
New Zealand (a division of Pearson New Zealand Ltd.) • Penguin Books (South Africa)
(Pty.) Ltd., 24 Sturdee Avenue, Rosebank, Johannesburg 2196, South Africa

Penguin Books Ltd., Registered Offices: 80 Strand, London WC2R 0RL, England

First published by Hudson Street Press, a member of Penguin Group (USA) Inc.

First Printing, May 2009
10 9 8 7 6 5 4 3 2 1

Copyright © Matthew Biberman, 2009
Vincati logo designed by Neal Videan and Phil Pilgrim. Used by permission from the creator.
All rights reserved

REGISTERED TRADEMARK—MARCA REGISTRADA
HUDSON
STREET
PRESS

LIBRARY OF CONGRESS CATALOGING-IN-PUBLICATION DATA

Biberman, Matthew, 1966–
    Big Sid's Vincati : the story of a father, a son, and the motorcycle of a lifetime / Matthew
Biberman.
        p. cm.
    Includes bibliographical references.
    ISBN 978-1-59463-053-8 (alk. paper)
    1. Biberman, Matthew, 1966–   2. Biberman, Sid, 1930–   3. Fathers and sons—United
States.   4. Mechanics (Persons)—United States—Biography.   5. Motorcyclists—United
States—Biography.   6. Home-built motorcycles—United States.   7. Motorcycles—
Customizing—United States.   8. Norfolk (Va.)—Biography.   9. Louisville (Ky.)—
Biography.   I. Title.
    CT275.B56734A3 2009
    975.5'521043092—dc22
    [B]   2008051162

Printed in the United States of America
Set in Electra   •   Designed by Eve L. Kirch

This book is printed on acid-free paper. ∞

FOR LUCY

Who insists that this book be called:
Big Sid's Vincati: The Story of a Grandfather, a Father,
and the Daughter of a Lifetime

Oh, we all like motorcycles to some degree
                                    —*Bob Dylan*

Fuelie heads and a Hurst on the floor
She's waiting down in the parking lot
Outside the 7-11 store
                                    —*Bruce Springsteen*

Said Red Molly to James that's a fine motorbike
                                    —*Richard Thompson*

Contents

Contents

Prologue: In the Hospital

I sit with my father in the emergency room while the doctors tell him what he has already guessed—he has had a heart attack. The admitting physician says that the extent of the damage is still unknown, and we will need to see a specialist. After they do the paperwork to transfer him from the ER to cardiac, I'm asked if I have a preference for a heart man.

I don't know any doctors in Louisville. I say, "It's in God's hands." The physician nods and assigns my dad, Sid, to the next available surgeon in the rotation. I am told that he will have his bypass surgery the next morning.

Alone at home that night, I can't help but feel weighted down by guilt. For the past twenty years, my father has barely been a part of my life. I fall asleep, fully expecting him to die.

But the next morning, five hours after they wheel him away, the surgeon tells me Sid is now in stable condition and should regain consciousness. He may be unconscious for a while, though, and I can go home until they call me. Still I ask to see him.

Prologue: In the Hospital

While listening to the wheeze of the ventilator, I reach down and squeeze Sid's hand. His unconscious, immobile body lies there draped in a sea green gown that is woefully inadequate in size. When I was tying it up in the ER, I examined the vast expanse of his back, slashed and pockmarked from past surgeries. The soft flesh was a mottle of different shades of brown, each splotch the result of some crash or accident. Sleeping, he looks at peace and grandly indifferent to the world. His last look at me before they rolled him away had been far different: terror mixed with acceptance.

Now I watch his eyes calmly move under his lids, and the sight calms me. His feet hang off the bed. He needs a haircut. His salt-and-pepper crown of hair stands up crazily. As I linger, the smell of industrial antiseptic solvents mixed with sweat grows stronger. After squeezing Sid's hand once more, I leave.

Time passes. Back at school, my lectures on Shakespeare roll out of my mouth in a robotic monotone. I forget to hang my parking card, and the campus police tow my car. I tell no one the reason for my distraction. And then the call comes: Sid is awake and off the ventilator.

Soon after, I sit beside him again and the first thing he says is, "Why didn't they just let me die?"

I know he means it, and for the first time, I realize why he didn't call me after suffering his heart attack. When I climbed those stairs that day and let myself into his ramshackle apartment, I found him waiting to die. The previous night we had watched a movie. I had promised that I would stop by in the morning, but instead slept in. Not wanting to apologize (after all, I was no kid and in no mood to be kept on a short leash), I hadn't called. Instead I had simply pulled up unannounced and hours late, expecting to take him to lunch. It was a beautiful Sunday afternoon in September. I opened the door and saw him, sunk in his one good chair, grasping a pillow, pressing it tight to his chest.

There wasn't time to think as I raced him to the ER. But now there was. What to say? How do you comfort a man disappointed at still being alive? That's when I began to put it all together. A few months earlier, when Sid moved from Norfolk, Virginia, to Louisville, it had not been to start a new life but to end, on his own terms, the only life God gives you.

As we talk, his eyes transfix me: endless black pools. It looks like he wants to sink into the bed to be covered over in the soft earth. You'd never know that the man lying there was a legend, one of the best motorcycle tuners in the country, if not the world. From all over, riders came with their bikes in tow. I would wake to find strange men, often from foreign lands who spoke little English, wanting to know if this house was where Big Sid lived. Sometimes they wanted to stay and just watch my father fix motorcycles, but Sid never liked to work with the spotlight on him. Like any good magician, he had earned the right to his own secrets.

When Sid was young, riding his red Vincent Rapide, he liked to play a game with guys who thought they were fast on their motorcycles. He would pull alongside, bolt upright, catching his prey. The other rider was feeling full of himself, the spark of life shining in his eyes as he hugged the tank of his Harley, or Triumph. And then suddenly there sat Big Sid, six feet five, three hundred pounds, as comfortable as can be on top of his Vincent. Sid would lean over and yell, "Have ya got it all on?" Then the game would commence, and it had only one ending: Sid would shift into fourth gear, wind it out, and vanish up the road. Sometimes as he pulled away he'd glance over to see their expression: that same shattered face I saw there in the hospital.

When Sid has his heart attack, I am three years into my job as an English professor. I had thought I was on a secure career path, but now, with little to show for it in the way of publications, I am facing the very real possibility that soon I might not be granted tenure. And no tenure means no job. My wife, Martha, and I are also trying to start a family, and she has just told me she thinks she might be pregnant. Suddenly, the prospect of taking care of her, plus two other family members—one old, one new—strikes me, there in that hospital room, as almost too unbearable to contemplate.

My mother had predicted it all. With Sid in Louisville, she said, I was about to get engulfed in my father's physical collapse: the knees were going; the back was shot; and, of course, the heart. The looming financial burden reminds me why I had been so adamant about running away from Sid's world. Someone once said that motorcycles are the best way to take a large fortune and turn it into a small one. In my father's case, his youthful joyriding had given way to the endless grind of running a motorcycle shop. The fame he had inadvertently accrued was of the purest sort, coming always with honor and never with money; his old racing wins were nothing but talk and a collection of half-broken trophies, most stashed in boxes in the attic. The comedian Jay Leno put it well when he told me that in a perfect world guys like my dad would be the ones living in the big houses. No surprise, then, that from age eighteen on I was terrified that I'd end up like Sid: broke and at the mercy of life.

And Sid knows what I feared. In his bed, he looks up at me almost as if to say, "It's okay to say good-bye, son." With no clue what to do, I mouth back empty words neither of us believe. Then I tell him to get some sleep and I slip out of the room. Convinced I need to do better next time I visit, I drive over to his apartment and rummage around, looking for pictures and magazines, anything that might help him find the will to live.

The following night I am back in the hospital, sitting next to his bed, holding up the pictures I had grabbed so that Sid can examine each one closely in the dim, off-white hospital light. I progress through the stack until I am faced with a motorcycle I can't identify. "What's that?" I ask.

He peers at it. "It's a Vincati. A Vincent motor in a Ducati frame. I saw one years ago at a rally."

I look at the picture again while making sense of this new word: *Vincati*. It's a recent shot, taken during bike week at the Isle of Man in 1999. One of Sid's British biker buddies had sent it to him, just one snapshot in a big stack, mostly of interesting machines spied here and there around the island. Exactly the sort of package Sid and his pen pals have been sharing with each other for over half a century.

Sid always describes himself as a motorcyclist and not a biker, by which he means he loves all kinds of motorcycles—and not just American iron. And he has passed that attitude on to me, especially when it comes to Italian bikes. He owned several Ducatis; they were his second love after British-made Vincents. While looking at the picture, I hear in my mind the peculiar loping chuckle of the Vincent's exhaust note. And then I think about how much I once loved the way a seventies-era Ducati chassis sits: long and relaxed, perfectly suited for a big twin motor. As a boy of seven, I had ridden behind my father on the first Ducati he ever owned. Then later, in the mid-eighties, a Ducati was my first true road bike, one that had come Big Sid's way as a sixty-dollar salvaged wreck. For me, the memories of those rides remain fresh and visceral in all their sights and sounds: a blur of plowed fields dotted with telephone poles, the smell of wood smoke, the sting of the wind, and, above all, the thunderous sounds of the exhaust pipes. Sid, riding alongside, still young enough to enjoy thrashing his Vincent Black Shadow. And me, stupid enough to "level peg" (as he likes to call it) with him at 80, 90, 100, 110 mph. Each of us looking across and nodding at the other.

Now in his drab hospital room, I stare at the photo of the Vincati. Then I look at my father. I feel a wave of excitement come over me.

"Did you ever build one?" I ask, slipping into the voice I use with students when they need encouragement.

"No." His voice croaks, still raspy and hollow from the ventilator. I had hoped he would catch my hint.

I try again. "Ever know anyone who did?"

"Why?" He says flatly, but then he senses my true meaning. "You? You want to build one?" His face freezes in shock. He knows as well as I do that this is something I could never do on my own.

"No, not me," I say. "Us. I was thinking we could build one together."

Now he looks stern—angry, and I know why. Sid has been waiting my whole adult life for me to ask him to do something like this, to work with him and learn all he knows about motorcycles. But when I finally do ask, it's too late: he's convinced he's dying. But maybe he is wrong about that.

I push harder. "But together we could. When you get out of here."

He laughs bitterly. "I'm finished."

"No you're not. You've got to try. Think about it. This bike would be something special."

The anger ebbs from his face. He realizes I'm serious.

"Imagine riding it," I add. At that moment nothing could seem more unlikely, and yet listening to myself, I suddenly feel convinced that it's possible, if I can only get him to believe.

I see him struggling with my suggestion. He has done pretty much everything you could do to a Vincent but he has never built a Vincati. No one outside of a handful of men in Australia had.

Then I see the hint of a smile, and I know that I have him hooked. Now he is the one with questions, real ones.

"So where are we going to build it? Certainly not in that cellar garage of yours. And where do we come up with the money?"

I tell him not to worry about those things, mere details. But in truth I have no idea. It all feels unreal, as if I am talking to a dead man about a dream.

Part One

How Sid Got Big

A good machinist always breaks the edge.

—Jake

Chapter One

Flat Out

The ocean draws men to its shore. There the sound of sea swell, the salt smell, and the sight of birds banking lazily overhead inspire dreams of travel. Men pick up tools and build boats and planes and cars—vehicles to take them faster and higher. This nurturing bond between the creative spirit and the sea helps explain why so many motorcyclists hail from port cities.

Norfolk, Virginia—Sid's hometown—is one such port city. Born in 1930, Sid was the second of Joe and Yetta Biberman's three sons. A Pole, Joe served in the German merchant marine shortly after the end of World War I. His sailing career came to an end when he jumped ship at Norfolk. There he opened a butcher shop, Joe's Meat Market, on Church Street, and married Yetta Epstein, the daughter of well-to-do Jews from Russia. Beautiful and glamorous, she sported the town's first fur coat. Initially the couple was happy, with Joe lavishing affection and expensive gifts on his wife as his business prospered. Sid's earliest years were peaceful and pleasant.

But as Joe became more successful, he began to crave the freedom and pleasures that new money made possible. Soon he had made a name for himself as a man's man, and a ladies' man too. As his boys grew up, my grandfather put them to work in his store so that some day he could count on them to run things, leaving him free to roam and do as he wished. Sid's older brother, Marvin, was slight, so my grandfather groomed him to be the bookkeeper. He treated his youngest son, Leonard, as a trophy child and always spoke of him as bound for medical school. But from the start, Joe had something else in mind for Sid. Here was a child well on his way to becoming a six-foot-five, three-hundred-pound hulk, and to Joe that meant free manpower. Hence college was off-limits to Sid.

Once Sid turned thirteen, Joe welcomed him to manhood in his own inimitable way. At Yetta's urging, Sid had a bar mitzvah, but Joe devised a plan for showing everyone what he really thought of that ceremony. On the Saturday when Sid was called for the first time to stand before the congregation, Joe chose instead to open his store and sell meat. Furious, Yetta dispatched a friend to retrieve her husband, who dutifully made his way straight to the temple without changing his clothes. The sight of Joe standing at the back of the sanctuary still in his bloody butcher's smock made a lasting impression on all. This calculated display of cruel thoughtlessness illustrates how Sid's father controlled his family. Indeed the only time I can remember seeing my grandfather smile was under similar circumstances.

Years later, when I was about to turn seven, I told Joe it was my birthday. He looked at me, feigning joyful surprise, and then in his heavily accented English spat out the words, "I wouldn't give you nothing." In that moment, I encountered real human cruelty for the first time. It was slight, but infinitely suggestive, and it hit me like a fist in the gut. Having dried my eyes on my mother's dress, I turned

4

around and glared back at my grandfather. He had buried the hook of hatred deep in me. Then I watched his lips curl into a smile of twisted satisfaction.

Growing up, my father must have seen that sick smile often. Shortly after Sid's bar mitzvah, Joe put him to work lugging sides of beef into the back of a large, long station wagon. Afterward Sid, covered in sweat, would sit silently next to his father in the front seat while Joe did his runs to Norfolk's restaurants. But Sid did have one escape.

As they traveled, he would gaze longingly out the passenger window, and whenever he spotted a young man riding a motorcycle, all his aches and pains would fall away and in his mind he would be zooming off on one of his own. While Joe drove, Sid would note the different bike shops that were springing up around town. At the end of the day, he would beg off the ride home and instead hoof it back to the bike shops he had spotted.

Soon Sid had visited them all, places like Bew's Harley on Fourth Street. Cold and cavernous, Bew's was lined with the stored bikes of sailors out on deployment. Closer to home—but hidden away—was Pop Gaus's Indian shop. You had to duck up an alleyway off Granby Street to get to it. A little later Sid discovered a new shop, Meridian Sales, at the head of that same alley. The place was run by two buddies fresh out of the navy, Shorty Sadler and Red Nabors, who had decided to stay near their old ship base and sell bikes. During Sid's visits, Shorty would tell war stories, of kamikazes hitting his ship while the fleet was softening up Okinawa.

But by far, Sid's favorite shop was Givens's Indian Sales and Service. To this day Sid remembers the first time he peered into the windows at the gleaming Chiefs. Once inside, a sinewy and powerful man a few years older than Sid glanced up at him before returning to the magazine he was reading. He was old man Givens's son, Gerald, who everyone called GG. Sid walked around the showroom floor, stopping in front of the biggest bike on display. It was clearly old and used but it sparkled. Sid looked it over, delighting in the Indian's white-wall tires, its individual treads shaped into the word "nonskid" like some massive round stamp, its big *ah-ouga* horn, and its large "suicide" clutch and tank-side shift knob.

GG looked again at the young teenager, seemed to make a decision, then stood up and walked over to Sid.

"Hell, kid," he said dismissively, "that's an old man's bike. You want to see something that can really go? Okay then, come with me."

GG led Sid past signs that read CUSTOMERS KEEP OUT, into the first proper workshop the teen had ever set foot in.

"Now that's a boy's racer," GG said as he stood before the shop's Indian Sports Scout. "Clipped all Bew's Harleys on that."

Sid swallowed hard and nodded.

"Go ahead," GG said. "Sit on it."

As Sid climbed up, he knew he would never forget that moment. A real race bike! Out on the street, all the guys said GG was unbeatable on it.

"Almost, kid," he heard GG say. "Another year or so and you'll be ready."

Sid hopped off and then GG fell to one knee to point out the various modifications he had made. From that day forward, GG became Sid's hero and that shop his mecca.

He promised GG that he would be back soon, ready to buy.

"Sure, kid," GG said, "by then the war will be over and we'll have a fleet of new Indians in here."

Shortly after that visit, Sid spotted an old heavy-duty Schwinn bicycle propped against a tree in front of a neighbor's house. The old man who lived there was struggling to clean out his basement. Sid stopped, and in exchange for lugging his junk out to the curb he got the bike.

Then with his bar mitzvah money, Sid bought a Whizzer kit at a little lawn and garden shop called Cuthrel's not far from his house. A Whizzer was a flathead motor that could be added to any full-size men's bicycle. In the evenings, after dinner, Sid worked out in the garage, attaching that motor to the Schwinn.

A week or so later, on a beautiful early spring day, he rolled the Whizzer out to the street, started it up, and took his first ride. To Sid the acrid exhaust smelled like perfume and the initial sensation was as thrilling as those hesitant dance steps a boy takes with his first girl. After a few puttering passes, Sid grew in confidence. Soon he was roaring along, enraptured by the experience of moving effortlessly through space, banking from left to right as he soared around bends.

A short time later, Sid stumbled upon his first trick to increase a motor's performance. One day, while looking over his bike, his eyes came to rest on the thick fiber gasket under the Whizzer's cylinder head. Why did the piece have to be so thick? After all, a gasket is simply material slipped between mating parts to prevent oil seepage. Sid removed the head and traced the outline of the existing gasket onto an aluminum pie pan, cut it out, and fit his homemade replacement in place of the original. The thinner aluminum allowed the head to be drawn farther down onto the cylinder, thus reducing the space of the combustion chamber, an alteration that Sid reasoned would make for more powerful detonation. It worked like a charm. Now, as a result of his alteration, that Whizzer went faster, and Sid was hooked on tuning.

Eventually, he traded his Whizzer for a Salsbury scooter. Sid discovered this wondrous device while out on a delivery run with Joe. He was hauling beef into a restaurant kitchen on Twenty-first Street, in Norfolk, when he spied a new Salsbury dealership. While his father was settling up, he wandered just far enough to stare in through the glass at a row of new shiny red scooters. The next time Sid stopped in, he left his Whizzer in trade and rode away on a Salsbury.

Soon he was racing it against his new friends—other Salsbury boys—who were all older, but always smaller. Though only fourteen, Sid already stood over six feet tall and weighed 250 pounds. It was the spring of 1945 and the war was winding down. The Germans had surrendered on May 8 and the Japanese were soon to follow. Everyone was ecstatic at the prospect of peace. It was a time when nobody seemed to mind kids buzzing up and down the street.

In the midst of one of their regular race sessions, Sid heard a dramatic knocking sound, clearly coming from the bottom end of his motor. A great drop in power followed, and then the bike began to shake as never before. In that instant, Sid knew there had been a major failure. He had pushed his machine too hard. It just couldn't sustain such speed, not with his weight on it.

After nursing the wounded Salsbury all the way home, Sid rounded up what tools he could find and launched into his first major teardown. He quickly discovered the problem: metal shards in the bottom of the motor. He could see what his hard riding had done: the rod's big end bearing had been pounded out. It was a case of "worn mains," which was what Jake down at Adesso Precision called it.

A gruff old man, Jake first told Sid to come back in a couple of hours and to bring thirty bucks. That was a lot of money to Sid, but every boy he knew swore by Jake. And Sid had spent enough time around such sour men that he paid the tone no mind. Instead he peeled off three tens. Then he offered to go around the corner and buy a package of smokes if he could stay.

When Sid returned, Jake found him a beat-up squat stool. Sid sat, perched quietly, and watched Jake melt the bearing material he called "Babbitt" and pour the rod. He turned the crank smooth before making the rod and the journal a perfect fit. Having warmed up to his young customer, he said, "A big boy like you is gonna have to learn some hop-up tricks." That afternoon Sid got some good advice on how to rebuild his scooter so that it could carry his weight and go fast. And from that first conversation, Sid fell in love with all the gearhead lingo. When he went home with his freshly rebushed flywheel assembly, he also knew how he was going to hop up his Salsbury: he'd channel the flathead block, and polish and enlarge the ports and the intake manifold too.

Once he had her running again, Sid went hunting. Spot a kid on a scooter. Saddle up alongside. And if the road was clear (or clear enough), they'd exchange looks, and then Sid would whack open the throttle and that was it: good-bye, Charlie. It wasn't a race; it was a good old-fashioned clipping, just like GG said, again and again, until eventually, when they saw Sid coming, the other boys would spin around and ride off in the other direction.

Now Sid grew bored with his Salsbury. He knew the time had come: he wanted a real motorcycle. But he did not take the investment lightly. When he stopped in at Henderson's, the local magazine and smoke shop, he spent his time paging through *Popular Mechanics*, all the latest car repair books, and, of course, the bike mags, especially the two British weeklies: *Motor Cycle* and *Motorcycling*. It was the spring of 1948 and the news was all about the '48 Earls Court Motorcycle Show in London, the first since the war. Flipping through the program, Sid felt sharp pains of lust as he stared at all the offerings from Ariel, Triumph, BSA, Norton, Sunbeam, and the rest.

But he stopped turning pages when he got to Vincent. Its Rapide, he learned, had been unveiled the previous year. In its first road test, the reviewers had listed the bike's top speed as "unobtainable." And as if that wasn't enough, the big news for '48 was Vincent's splashy intro-duction of an even faster model, the Black Shadow. Philip Vincent had promised reporters that this one would deliver an unthinkable 125 mph or better, straight out of the box. To a boy such as Sid who had barely seen 65 mph, such speeds seemed so outlandish as to be unreal, something out of the *Amazing Stories* magazines he had once devoured.

As much as Sid loved to read about great bikes, what he valued most was riding. He was never the kind of guy who was willing to save his pennies and spend his time fantasizing about the day when he had enough to buy some dream machine. Instead he cashed in his war bonds and began haunting Givens's and the rest of the shops—Meridian Sales and Pop Gaus's—ready to buy the best bike he could get right then for the money in his pocket.

He settled on a new Matchless Super Clubman, which he found in yet another new shop, English Motorcycle Sales, operating out of an old hangar at the Portsmouth Airport. A 500 cc vertical twin, the Clubman was an instant delight in design and beauty, with its chromed and paneled tank, dual seat, and sturdy swing-arm rear frame. The tank's accent color was a soft deep orange with a reddish tinge. But the real jewel was its lovely center-main-bearing motor, so elegantly shaped and polished like quicksilver. Sid included his Salsbury in the trade.

As he pulled away on his first real motorcycle, Sid felt incredible.

He sped out of town and into the peanut fields outside Suffolk and couldn't imagine that he could ever want more out of life.

Now Sid spent many afternoons hanging out at GG's shop. GG always treated him warmly, though Sid felt guilty about buying his bike elsewhere. But GG never said anything about it. Still, Sid made an effort to buy accessories from his hero and to help out around the shop when he could.

One afternoon Sid was helping GG tune a recent shipment of new bikes: GG was never satisfied with how the factory set them up—he had mastered the art of proper carburetion and Sid was eager to learn. When the mail came, they took a break. GG called Sid over to show him the latest issue of *Cycle*. It had news from Bonneville.

Since as far back as 1911, racers had traveled to Bonneville, a desolate stretch of dry lake bed, to do one thing: go fast. With time what began as simple joyriding developed into the serious sport of land speed racing, in which the goal is to achieve the highest speed possible over a long straight course.

Sid took the magazine from GG. A Vincent Black Shadow piloted by the veteran racer Rollie Free had just set a new American mark for motorcycles. Dressed only in swim trunks and a bathing cap, to cut down on weight and wind drag, Free had achieved a mean two-way average of 150.313 mph, smashing the previous mark by nearly 15 mph. Gazing at the now-famous picture of Free lying flat out on the bike, Sid knew that in this case the manufacturer's claims were true: the Vincent was the most powerful bike in the world.

In the summer of 1950, Sid was out for a Sunday afternoon ride near "the five-mile stretch," a favorite road on which to race, when he heard the unmistakable sound of another motorcycle closing in from behind. Suddenly, something strange appeared alongside, with a sound he had never heard before. The rider wore an aviator's cap and large goggles, the common gear of the day. The bike was all black.

Sid was stunned. Then he recognized it: that fabulous machine he had only read about—a Vincent Black Shadow. He looked up at the owner to fix the face of this lucky son of a bitch, the first in the Tidewater region to own one of what the British press was calling "the Kings of the Road." The other rider caught Sid's eye and smiled, and that's when Sid placed the face—it was "Mac" McCowan, already one of Sid's closest riding buddies. It was the Vincent that had thrown him. Mac's usual bike was a slate blue 650 Triumph Thunderbird.

What was *he* doing on a Black Shadow?

Mac smiled again and began to tease Sid, rolling the throttle on before easing off to allow Sid to catch up. Then Mac leaned over and uttered a taunt common among bikers back then. Slowly, in his Southern drawl he asked, "Ya got it all on?"

Sid responded by racking the throttle against the stop in top gear and falling forward to hug the tank. For an instant he felt he was alone and that Mac had fallen behind. Then that damn Vincent flashed past and vanished into the distance.

Sid listened in shock as within the roar of the wind he heard the sound of Mac's bike shifting from third into fourth! His buddy hadn't even been in top gear. It was like being passed by a rocket ship.

Awestruck, Sid rode on in the hopes of spotting this incredible machine again. Several miles later, he saw the bike and rider parked by the side of the road. Sid shot past and then circled around before pulling to a stop.

Mac was enjoying a cigarette while Sid put his bike on its stand

and walked over for his first examination of a Vincent Black Shadow. To Sid it looked somber and pretty as brass knuckles—far different from his gaudy Matchless. Side by side, the two bikes were about the same length, with tanks and seats, but there, where the engines sat, was the major difference. The Vincent's motor was twice the size and yet crammed into the same physical space. To Sid it was like staring at a wrestler who stood before you with his chest boldly thrust outward. In contrast, the Matchless's engine now seemed puny.

The Shadow's owner, Mac, was a few years older than Sid, and a roughneck ringer for Gary Cooper.

"I do believe I clocked you doing ninety-five back there, Sid," Mac said.

"How fast will that Vincent go?" Sid said, still stunned at the memory of the machine vanishing up the road.

"No idea." Mac laughed. "I asked the previous owner, and he didn't want to learn. That's why he sold it."

"How long have you had it?" Sid asked.

"I'm just riding it home now."

The previous owner, Lester Perkins, had ridden it into town from Panama, where he picked it up from a Brit doing some work on the Canal. It may sound odd that he decided to get rid of the Vincent because it went *too* fast, but such a reaction was actually pretty common. Dealer feedback during the years of its production (1947–55) was a constant drumbeat for Vincent to stop touting performance and to stress, instead, what a great touring ride the bike was. Many potential sales were lost when the interested party simply chickened out, realizing, in the lingo of the day, that the Vincent was TFFO—too fast for owner. That clearly wasn't an issue for Sid, and he was thrilled when Mac offered him the chance to ride the Vincent himself.

Mac started the Shadow and then dismounted. Sid got on and set about familiarizing himself with all the controls while Mac hustled over to join him on the Matchless. Sid declutched and selected low gear, and together the two men pulled off. The Vincent's smooth, nonchalant manner impressed Sid instantly. It was as if he were being towed by some great elastic force while the trees rushed by. He could almost count the exhaust beats that composed the V-twin's massive offbeat rhythm. He felt little of the constant vibration experienced on every other bike he'd ever ridden, and the suspension coped with road conditions perfectly, tracking straight and true.

Chancing a rearward glance, Sid saw Mac smile and, with a nod of the head, motion him to "have a go" as they turned back onto the five-mile stretch. Already in third, Sid rolled on the throttle and slid farther back, while gripping the tank between his knees. In a few seconds, he pulled past eighty, where, with clenched teeth, he momentarily eased in the clutch and thrust into top gear. The air rushed in a torrent around his helmet as he steadily increased his speed.

Sid stole a glance down at the huge speedometer: 100 mph plus! And he still had plenty of throttle in hand. With that moment came the full realization of how motors go about producing power. At that speed, the little Matchless's exhaust wailed out a single high-pitched note as its pistons flew up and down. Not the Vincent. Even at 100 mph, you could hear the thud of each power stroke—*bam, bam, bam*—like measured fists to an opponent's face thrown by a boxer with an endless reserve of punches.

For Sid this ride was a life-changing event. As he eased off the throttle, he thought again of what Rollie Free had done: run 150 mph. Now all over the world, speed marks were being eclipsed by men on Vincents.

Finally, Sid heard Mac pull up alongside. As the two men cruised together, Sid felt as if he could almost step off and walk. And that's when it hit him: this machine really had changed everything. This very bike he was riding was just as capable as the one ridden by Rollie Free, and from that moment forward Sid wanted to set a record of his own.

After the two men swapped machines and nodded their good-byes, Sid remounted his Matchless. Suddenly, it had shrunk in stature, power, and meaning.

But Sid soon learned that getting his dream bike was not going to be easy. At Sid's urging, the bike shop owners all made inquiries but without success. In 1950 a Vincent cost over a thousand dollars, making it three or four hundred dollars more than most other motorcycles. But when you talk to bikers from that era, it's clear that there were willing customers like my father all over America. So Vincent did not go out of business because the bikes were too expensive. Rather it was mostly a matter of poor distribution.

Sid wasn't the only convert among his crowd. Mac's new Shadow also worked its magic on two other bikers—Willie Wooten and Johnny Marshall—and these men were as ready and willing as my father to go anywhere in North America to collect a Vincent. On New Year's Eve, Sid and his friends even made a bet on who would be the first to claim the prize. As they raised their glasses high to ring in 1951, Sid felt certain he would be the last to strike gold.

Then one afternoon in late February, Sid's luck turned. He rolled up to Givens's Indian Sales, looking to kill some time on a break from work and to see his friend GG. As he walked into the back of the shop that day, Sid stumbled on a most unusual sight: half a dozen large crates.

GG told him that they contained bikes to be displayed at an up-coming spring hot-rod show and asked if Sid wanted to help uncrate them. Sid selected the largest one. After pulling off a few slates, Sid let out a whoop: inside was a red Vincent. His hands shook and his mouth went dry as he carefully uncovered this treasure. Assembly was simple: the muffler needed to be slipped on and the handlebar bolted in place.

But first Sid had to convince Gerald to sell him the bike. Finally, Sid could make good on that promise to buy from him. Yet even as Sid readily agreed to all of GG's conditions, he sensed that somehow his old hero didn't really want him to have the bike. Nevertheless Sid pushed on and the deal was struck. The Matchless went and damn near every cent too. The only proviso was that the bike had to be displayed in the show before Sid officially took possession of it.

Sid then learned from Gerald how the Vincent arrived there in the first place. Indian's sales were faltering, so the company had decided to become the face of the surging British invasion. The Vincent was included in this deal and the Black Shadow was given prominent placement in the ads, but not in the shipping schedules. Norton, Matchless, and Royal Enfield—examples of all these brands soon became plentiful. But not Vincents. Perhaps Indian still dreamed of fielding its own big twin and resuming its rivalry with Harley. Whatever the case, Vincents would remain hard to find in America, and in his more generous moments my father imagined that the new coldness he sensed in GG could be attributed to those lost sales.

Sid knew he had gotten incredibly lucky that afternoon, and he was ready to leave on his Vincent immediately. But first he had to walk back outside and roll in his faithful Matchless while GG held open the door. Sid felt guilty about abandoning his first real motorcycle. And his instincts were proved right—GG promptly sold the bike, and the next time Sid saw the Clubman it was totaled, only the grips and polished fin edges allowed him to make the ID.

But what Sid really wanted was that Vincent. He rocked his red Rapide off the rear stand and walked it out of the store. Just beyond the shop doors, Sid gathered himself for the first ride home. The odometer showed twenty miles and he spotted an enigmatic chalked X on the seat base. With his first kick, the red Rap started and settled down immediately into a pleasant idle. The exhaust made a lovely burble, topped in richness only by the Burgess muffler commonly used on Triumphs.

Sid's heart was racing wildly as he pulled away. But then, just as quickly, the bike stalled at a light. Sid paddled out of traffic and then booted the kick-starter again and again until the motor caught. Sid lurched on only to stall it twice more. Each time, Sid's nerves got worse. To him, his Vincent felt skittish and unbroken—quite determined to buck him off. Exhausted and drenched in sweat, Sid felt lucky when he finally arrived safely home.

He made great strides during the next few days, riding around to show it off to his buddies. Mac was thrilled to have another Vincent in town, and Sid enjoyed pulling up in front of first Willie's and then Johnny's in order to relish having won their bet. Sid let each man have a go, and waited nervously until he heard the approaching exhaust of his baby.

By the time Sid rode over to the arena for the hot-rod show, as promised, he had broken in the grabby clutch. Sid kept a constant eye on the Rapide at the show, as if he were a jealous husband and it a faithless wife. Much to Sid's chagrin, the show attracted many young children. It was torture for Sid to watch the young kids play with the throttle and stand on the exhaust pipe. The Rapide's leather seat got scuffed, but that wasn't the worst of it. At one point, a father carelessly rested his baby on the tank for a picture, and the boy's dangling shoes scratched the paint.

Finally, Sid reclaimed his treasure and set out for home. On the ride, he dreamed of all the modifications he would make, and all the places he would go and the adventures that awaited him.

A few days later, he received his draft notice in the mail.

Chapter Two

Last Train to London

Before leaving Norfolk, Sid decided to store his bike at Meridian. The shop was close to home, and he really trusted the owner, Shorty. Sid still admired GG, but ever since he bought the Vincent he sensed their friendship had cooled, so he looked elsewhere for his bike's caretaker. Nor was he thrilled to have learned that GG had allowed his Matchless to fall into the hands of a wild sailor who then promptly wrecked it. Shorty promised Sid he would run his Rapide occasionally and keep it in good shape.

After reporting for induction at Fort George G. Meade in Maryland, Sid was issued a uniform so absurdly small that he couldn't even sit in it. They just didn't have anything on hand for a man who stood six feet five inches and weighed 280 pounds. He was sent on to basic training with the 101st Airborne at Camp Breckenridge, Indiana, just over the Ohio River from Louisville. For the first two weeks he drilled in civies, right down to his size 15EEE shoes, practically destroying all his clothes.

In an early conversation with an officer, Sid mistakenly volunteered

19

the information that he was a butcher, and was promptly assigned to the kitchen detail. He soon found the task physically unbearable—he couldn't stand the smell of raw seafood. Even worse, he hoped to use the army to learn a different trade: he still dreamed of getting out from under his father. But the army figured differently, and the prospect of coming back even better trained to run Joe's Meat Market angered him. In a frenzy, Sid intentionally hacked up sides of beef, turning them into hamburger and destroying the knives in the process. After that, his CO gave Sid what he wanted: a transfer to engineering. There he enjoyed himself as he learned how to work on military vehicles.

After basic training, Sid was assigned to Europe. This was a lucky break as the other option was Korea, which would have likely meant combat. For the remainder of his hitch, Sid was stationed with a unit of army engineers in the little town of Ettlingen, Germany, where he labored on ten-wheel, six-ton dump trucks, powered by huge International engines. There he kept a small notebook, where he carefully drew up a list of Vincent Black Lightning parts to buy to help him with his planned modifications.

While overseas, Sid dreamed of visiting the Vincent works in Stevenage, England, and in early October 1953 he got his chance. Armed with a weekend pass, he made the trip to the U.K. sitting in a jump seat aboard a U.S. government courier plane. Sid arrived in London to find brilliant autumn weather, quite unlike the rain and fog he was expecting from all that he'd read.

Though born in Fulham, England, in 1908, Philip Vincent was raised in Argentina, on his father's cattle ranch. When the young boy was sent back to England for prep school, he fell under the spell of motorcycles. First he bought a BSA, but then quickly traded it for an ABC. Utterly disappointed by the performance of both, Vincent decided that he could build a better motorcycle himself, and by the time he had matriculated at Cambridge to study engineering he was gallivanting about on his own innovative machine.

Vincent rapidly came to dislike Cambridge, finding its culture both complacent and risk averse, so he dropped out and started his own motorcycle company. After a little advance planning, he and his managing director, Frank Walker, founded the factory in Stevenage. Twenty-five years later, Sid was walking toward that very spot.

The Vincent works was only a short walk down Hitchin Road. Sid had taken a train out from London. He exited the station, crossed a small bridge, and shortly saw the "new works" at Fishers Green, a building adjacent to Vincent's original facility. Sid looked over at a nearby field and saw a translucent white canvas tent. Outside it were rows of Vincents, with more bikes arriving by the minute. By some stroke of luck, Sid discovered, his visit had coincided with the annual Vincent Owners Club Rally. By the end of the day there would be more than two hundred club members and their bikes present.

Sid forgot all about his plan to order parts and wandered over to the tent instead. Inside he was surrounded by rare models, special factory projects, and race bikes, both solo and sidecar. He saw a rare Series A twin, a "sectioned" Series A Comet motor, and an ultrarare model W two-stroker, complete with leg shielding. To its right sat a Picador motor, a modified Vincent motorcycle engine developed to propel a drone aircraft, as well as another war ministry project, a Uniflo air-sea rescue lifeboat motor. Next Sid came across a very nicely detailed Black Lightning–based sidecar outfit. But it was the tent's center attraction that brought sweat to Sid's palms—the legendary works racer, Gunga Din. That bike held more records than any other machine in England, and quite possibly the world. Sid had only read about it in the magazines, where it was written that if regular rider George Brown wasn't flung off, he was just about sure to win.

Sid stood before Gunga Din slack jawed, trying to take in every detail and modification. He even popped off the fuel cap and inhaled the methanol, eager to smell the fuel of a champion.

Seeing Gunga Din reminded Sid why he was there in the first place—to buy parts—so he left the tent and walked across the field.

Once inside the factory, he was cordially welcomed by Paul Richardson, the works' boffin. Paul served as Vincent's press secretary, and part of his job was to greet visiting customers and arrange for tours. On that day the factory wasn't open to all the club members— with the rally there were just too many—but Paul talked to Vincent and had Sid cleared for a tour because he was a visiting American soldier.

Alan Rennie was the guide. His main job was in the engine department. He took Sid on a captivating tour that passed through every assembly area. Sid was even offered a chance to ride a Vincent Firefly moped, and he accepted, taking the tiny, underpowered bike for a quick spin in the factory's back car park. All the while, Rennie chatted, passing along in great detail the Vincent story. Sid was especially keen to hear more about Vincent's head engineer, Phil Irving. Irving first developed Vincent's 500 cc single, the Comet, back in 1934. Then two years later, he experienced a serendipitous revelation: glancing down at his drafting board where two tracings of his single engine happen to lay in a V, he saw in a flash how to double up his design with little additional tooling cost. The result became Vincent's legendary twin.

Sid saw teams of men working to assemble Rapide engines. The production of all models was at its peak and hopes were high. He had always wondered how Vincents were painted, and there in the paint shed he stared at the large drums of black. They used a dipping process and then left the parts to hang from the rafters. (On some pieces he spotted runs.) Next he admired the machine used to bend pipes into the Vincent's unique two-into-one exhaust system.

For the grand finale, Sid watched a new Black Lightning being assembled by two men in white coveralls. This machine was different in that it was set up not just for racing but for the road, which meant it was fitted with lights, a generator, and a full complement of parking stands. Sid asked one of the men how fast this road-ready Black Lightning would be able to go. The man looked up from his check sheet. "If kept sharply tuned, it should top one forty." In that instant, Sid saw the future of his Rapide. It would be an awesome task, given how green he was, but he swore that nothing would stop him.

When the tour ended, Rennie asked Sid if he wanted to wash up before leaving. Sid declined, saying that he liked the feel of Vincent grease on his palms. Rennie was impressed. Sensing that Sid was a kindred spirit, he invited his guest to his house before that night's rally banquet over in Cambridge.

Rennie went to punch out and left Sid at the parts counter. Sid ordered four Shadow brake drums, Shadow carbs and manifolds, and a pair of Black Lightning cams. After making arrangements to have the parts shipped home, Sid headed back to Richardson's office to wait for Rennie.

On the way, he was stopped by Mr. Vincent himself, accompanied by Frida, his wife. "You must be our American owner!" Vincent exclaimed.

Sid showed the couple a color shot of his Rapide.

Vincent remarked, "Oh, you got one of the red ones. We only did twenty-four of those, and then we used the balance of the paint on my car." He pointed to a red Bristol sedan parked just across from the factory's doors.

When Vincent asked Sid about the tour, Sid told him he had seen his destiny—that the docile Rapide in the photograph was about to be transformed into a snarling Black Lightning. Vincent chortled and feigned surprise at encountering another American Vincenteer hell-bent on going fast. Taking the bait, Sid broke out his parts receipts. Vincent told Sid that as much as he appreciated Sid's enthusiasm, those parts alone would not make his bike a Black Lightning.

"Someday soon I'll order the rest," Sid pledged.

"I know you will, Yank," Vincent said patting him on the shoulder. "Make us proud."

That night at the banquet, the restaurant's main dining room echoed with the excited chatter of men, many clad in dark riding gear. Periodically, the conversation was drowned out as another covey of big twins rumbled up. Before dessert was served, Vincent stood and gave a few brief remarks in which Sid was introduced as the sole American member present. At Sid's table were Rennie and a few of his friends, including Steve Luff, who became one of Sid's best pen pals. The party wound down around one in the morning, and Sid asked Steve where he could catch the train back to London. Luff told him that the last train had already left.

Ben Chapman, another club member, overheard and interrupted, offering Sid a ride back to London on his tuned Shadow. Chapman was short yet powerfully built. He dressed in a thick fur-lined leather flying jacket, with matching long gloves and boots, worn over a pair of heavy-weight trousers.

Sid wore only his standard army dress uniform, his soft cap held to his head by a wool scarf (pinched from Rennie) tied under his chin. He was woefully underdressed for a fast midnight ride on a brisk October night. While he climbed on, he felt like the two of them must have looked like some ridiculous Laurel and Hardy act.

But this Vincent had no problem shouldering the load. Ben played the gearbox like twinkle toes attached to some 125 cc Ducati, never missing a shift. He kept the motor near full bore, as he hustled around those old British back lanes. Several times Sid stole a glance at the massive speedometer, dumbstruck and terrified to see it indicating speeds of near 120.

The road ahead was pitch-black, illuminated only by moonlight and the motorcycle's Miller electrics. The crisp air was tinged with wood smoke, and periodically Sid felt an intense coldness settle around him. All the while that great motor boomed out its throaty exhaust.

After what seemed like a never-ending roller-coaster ride, they reached London. The bike chuffed round Piccadilly Circus and over to Kensington as Ben slowed to a pleasant, sedate pace. As Sid gathered his thoughts, he realized that this feat had been astounding. He and Chapman dwarfed the Vincent—together the two men combined for well over 500 pounds. The bike, meanwhile, weighed only about 480, fully fueled. And yet the Shadow had cracked off 120 easily. Later Sid was to learn that on that very machine Chapman had recently set a new record for the famous run from Land's End to John o' Groat's (the southernmost tip of England to the farthest part of Scotland).

Chapman let Sid off within walking distance of his digs. As Sid watched Chapman vanish up the road, Vincent's words of encouragement echoed in his head: "Make us proud."

Chapter Three

A Score to Settle

Shortly before Christmas 1953, Sid returned from Germany. He took the train from Baltimore down to Norfolk, thinking the whole time about how excited he was to reclaim his Rapide and get started on all the necessary modifications. Still dressed in army fatigues, and even before he headed home, Sid stopped in at Meridian Sales to collect his bike.

In the intervening two years there had been some changes to the shop. For a start, it now sold Triumphs instead of BSAs. Shorty, who had promised to take care of the bike, was no longer the owner but simply the manager. Sid learned then that Meridian had been bought up by GG. Something in Shorty's expression made Sid nervous.

Sid wanted to know only one thing: Where was his Rapide?

"I'm gonna give it to you straight, Sid," Shorty said. And then he told Sid that one of the first things GG did was order Shorty to prep Sid's Vincent to drag race.

Sid looked at him, and Shorty dropped his head. "I did it, Sid. I'm sorry."

Shocked, Sid didn't respond for a few seconds.

Shorty added, "I got all your packages." He motioned to a stack of boxes. On top was a small box for his mother: a bottle of Chanel No. 5 packed in a clutch handbag.

"Where is my bike?" Sid asked again.

"Over at Givens's Indian shop. Down in the basement."

When Sid heard that, his heart froze. Norfolk is below sea level and in those days, with a good rain, downtown Norfolk was underwater.

"It wasn't even broken in," Sid said. "Did you go into her?"

Shorty shook his head. Sid's mind raced through a thousand scenarios. A drag start is a brutal act. Even one attempt can destroy a standard motor. Sid's anger was growing, but so was his shock.

Sensing a real problem, Shorty called over to the Indian shop. When he got off the phone, Shorty told Sid they were rolling his Vin out front.

"Sid," Shorty said, "my advice is just pick it up and go."

By the time Sid arrived, on foot, he was apoplectic. He saw his once beautiful red Rapide sitting on its side stand. It was intact, thank God, though covered in damp grime and corrosion. When Sid tried to kick-start it, he discovered that the lever was locked up, indicating that the motor had seized. He noticed that the pipes were blued and rusty at the headers. It was clear his baby had been through hell. He thought about storming into the store to confront GG.

But after a moment, he turned back around and began to walk his gutted bike home. He didn't know what he'd do to GG if he saw him, so he decided it was best to leave. But just then his friend-turned-enemy stepped out of the shop and the two men faced each other.

Frozen in rage and confusion, Sid just stared into his eyes.

GG sneered and said, "I know what a guy like you will tell the guys—you'll say I screwed you. Well, I could screw you worse." He opened his shop door, and just before he walked back inside, GG spat out, "But I'll tell you what I'm not: I'm no kike."

If Sid had had a gun, he might very well have shot GG. Instead he lit a cigarette and resumed walking his Rapide.

The march home allowed him to burn through his anger. It wasn't the first time he had been called a kike. But never before by someone who he had looked up to. Sid immediately blamed himself. He wondered what he had done to cause GG to do this.

Then while coasting down a hill toward home, he relaxed, relieved to feel that his Rap's chassis was still sound. It occurred to Sid then that maybe GG was angry at him because he had never brought him more customers. It was the best explanation he could hit upon, but down deep he knew there was never a sane reason for such hatred.

After a long struggle, Sid managed to push the bike into his garage. Then he walked inside the house. He surprised his mother, who ran across the kitchen and gave him a hug. He sat and talked with her, waiting for his father to come home. As that moment neared, Sid realized that he wanted to flee. He heard the door open and then his father walked in.

Joe hesitated for a moment. Then he said to his son, "Good to have you back."

Sid felt his father pat him on the shoulder and instantly knew Joe wanted him back at work in the store. Yetta brought Sid a stack of mail she had been saving for him. Joe vanished into the bedroom to change. Dinner would be on the table soon.

Sid thumbed through the mail slowly. Then he smiled when he

saw a letter from the Vincent Club. He quickly opened it and out slipped his membership card. He was still alive. His Rapide could be rebuilt. There were other ways to deal with GG.

Not long after that, Sid ordered all the parts he'd told Mr. Vincent he would someday buy. Thanks to Gerald's poor treatment of the Rapide, Sid simply had no choice. So there went that secret stash of cash he had been saving to put toward college. And someone would have to do all that work—a complete teardown, and there was no money for that. He would have to do it all himself.

But as much as Sid was afraid of the challenge, he was just as eager and happy to lose himself in it. Within a few sessions, he had the bike apart. Intense heat from repeated full-bore drag runs had partially melted the pistons, so Sid replaced them with a high-compression racing set. He also found rust throughout the motor's internals, no doubt the result of floodwaters.

At this point Sid discovered that the damage went beyond what he could ever hope himself to fix. Fortunately, when Sid returned, he had looked up Mac. His old riding buddy welcomed him home and, to Sid's delight, he still had his Vincent. Indeed he was into motorcycles even more deeply and was doing a lot of repair work out of his house. It was Mac who came to the rescue and did what Sid could not do: overhaul the lower end—just as Jake had years before.

Mac was like Jake in other ways too: gruff, with a weakness for drink. But Sid implicitly trusted him with his life. It was trust well placed. Point for point, Mac matched what the factory had done to make Gunga Din a legend.

Sid, though, was still not satisfied. Now his correspondence with his new Vincent Club friend Steve Luff served to his advantage. The two arranged a trade: Off to Steve went a "Yank" Bell helmet and—even more prized—a Langlitz police-style leather jacket. In exchange Luff sent Sid a brace of 32 mm TT racing carbs he managed to buy off George Brown, Gunga Din's pilot. Sid then ported—that is, opened up—the cylinder heads and polished and lightened the rockers and cam followers.

Now, two years after its purchase, that once docile Rapide became every bit the equal of the road-going Lightning Sid saw on his tour back in Stevenage. It was probably even a shade or two superior. The bike simply flew, and Sid was at last ready to execute his plan for revenge: he was going to whip GG's ass—out on the road, where it really mattered.

But it wasn't going to be easy. While Sid was toiling away on his Rapide, GG had been campaigning a new Triumph with great success. Employing every trick in the book, GG's full-house and lightened 650 sported 13½-to-1 pistons, racing camshafts, dual large-bore racing carburetors jetted for methanol fuel, and ran dual open megaphones. He had been easily whipping all comers. The window of his shop filled with trophies.

And his racing success didn't stop there. Just that spring at the 1956 Daytona drags, GG had posted the meet's top quarter-mile speed at 112.5 mph, a huge victory. None of this was a surprise to Sid. He had ridden down himself with his close friend, Bugs, a sailor who had turned up in Norfolk on his own Black Shadow. They went to watch Tommy McDermott finish fourth on his BSA Gold Star in the meet's grand event, the two-hundred-miler. Tommy raced out of Shorty's shop, and it was there that Sid and Bugs had befriended him. While down in Florida, Sid heard of the success GG was enjoying over at the Daytona drag strip but he refused to watch his enemy race.

It was several weeks after Daytona that Sid finally brought himself to walk back into GG's shop. All the Indian signs had come down, replaced by Triumph ones. Sid stood there and listened to GG boast to a group of guys about taking the field down in Florida.

"So after they gave me the trophy," GG said, "I told all the guys there to put their bikes on their trailers, and not to bring 'em back till they could pull the slack out of the rear chain."

When the laughter died down, Sid said, "Well then, I'll see you out at Suffolk this Sunday."

GG had seen Sid come in but didn't acknowledge him until Sid threw down this challenge. GG was slow to accept it: "I don't know, Sid. Depends on the weather. Might go to the strip. Might take in a picture."

"I got my Rapide together," Sid said.

"Did you, now?"

The two men exchanged looks. Then GG turned and walked into the back, where Sid had once felt so welcome. Sid stood stock still, consumed with anger. Then he turned and left.

The first nationally sanctioned drag races were held on April 11, 1953, in Pomona, California. The new sport employed a system of classes based on engine size and fuel. Two racers lined up side by side, and when the starter dropped his flag, the winner was the one who first crossed the finish line a quarter mile away. Soon similar tracks sprung up all over California: Lyons in Long Beach, Santa Ana, Saugus, and

Colton to name but a few. Quarter-mile strips then moved inland and opened on the East Coast as well. Battles between East and West became popular, followed by barnstorming tours, all while know-it-all engineers—Johnny Slide Rules—declared that there were immutable laws and the ceiling was such and such, only to see new marks set. Terminal speeds skyrocketed past 150 mph, and elapsed times fell below the ten-second mark and then well into the single digits.

When Sunday morning arrived, Sid hooked up a single-rail trailer behind his '56 "power pack" Chevy, loaded up the Rapide, and drove out to the Suffolk drag strip. He had no idea if GG would show up, but at least he could collect a few timing slips and make some tuning adjustments. Of course if Joe had his way, the shop would be open and his son would be behind the counter, but it was state law that all shops were closed on Sundays.

Naturally, Sid liked spending his Sundays out at the strip. That morning the sun rose, turning the sky a clear blue that made for perfect racing weather. As Sid settled in to the routine, he totally forgot about GG. It was just about joyriding.

At the main gate, Sid paid his fee and drove on in, looking for a place to pit.

Sid paused in his search and watched as a clean BSA Gold Star left the line. Its rider knew what he was doing: he kept both feet on the ground, while under him the bike lifted up as the real wheel began to spin in place. Then just as quickly it hooked up, gained traction, and down the track he sped. Sid drove on and finally found an open space. Moments later he was joined by the BSA rider who he had just watched run.

33

The guy's name was Paul Hall, and he was happy to share his pit with Sid. Sid began to fiddle with his Vincent. Then he heard the familiar wail of twin pipes nearby, and there was GG on that fearsome Triumph.

GG knew he had Sid's attention, and he then flicked his eyes toward the start line. Sid realized that he hadn't even brought proper riding gear and was dressed only in a short-sleeved shirt and wool slacks. Amazingly, he even had on dress shoes.

But none of that mattered. He started the Rapide with one fluid kick. It came to life, sounding sharp and ready.

"At least borrow my cap," Paul begged him. Sid put on the leather aviator's cap and rode to stage with GG. He blipped the throttle to clear the Rap's throat as he walked the bike up, keeping even with GG in the two lines that were making their way to the flagman who stood at the start. As they neared him, the combined roar of their motors grew deafening. Sid could not distinguish his own engine from all the rest, not even when he repeatedly revved the throttle, and without the sound to focus on, he realized he wasn't even wearing gloves.

From the moment the white flag fell, and Sid rolled on the throttle, everything went wrong. Sid was sitting too far back and the rear wheel was not breaking free to spin. He had been too heavy on the throttle and had let in the clutch too late. If a motorcycle's rear wheel can't begin to spin then disaster follows. The front wheel lurches forward and up—like a sprung mousetrap—and takes the bike into a backward flip. Sid's only option was to step off the bike before it ended up on top of him. While GG raced down the strip in a blur, Sid fell on his ass and bounced down the track. He watched in horror as his bike motored on ahead, riderless and on its rear wheel. He managed to get up and hobble over to his where his Rapide had finally come crashing to a halt. He saw immediately that the throttle and pipes were a little scarred, and he knew that he himself had a bad case of road rash, but that was the worst of it. He had lucked out. He got the Rapide up, started it, and somehow rode off back to the pits.

There GG was waiting for him, with a crafted expression of triumph on his face. He said, "You had enough?"

Sid looked at him. Then he turned around and kneeled before his bike, red faced and beaten. "That's it for today."

GG laughed. "Then bring it back when you can get it to pull the slack out of the rear chain!" He roared away toward the main gate and left.

Sid began to pack up to head home, Paul's aviator cap still on his head. He walked over to the BSA, where he found Paul staring in despair at his smoked clutch. Sid had been so out of it after his fall that he hadn't noticed that Paul had done another run, with an unfortunate result.

Sid held out the cap.

Paul took it back. "You need some help?"

"My ass must look as red as the rising sun," Sid cracked.

Listening to Paul's gentle laughter, Sid had an epiphany. Sure he had dreams of doing it all himself, of being a great tuner *and* a great rider, but if he was going to best GG, he needed to let that go. He needed someone else in the saddle. He had known that for a long time, but only now he was ready to act. Tuning—building and maintaining the bike—that was the work that really called to him.

Paul was thinking along the same lines. "Hey, Sid," he said. "Hasn't anybody told you? You're just too goddamn *big*. And your motorcycle is just too damn fast. Something's gotta give."

"Yeah," Sid said. Then he added, "Next time, would you ride it?"

"Hell yes," Paul said simply. He held out his hand, "I won't let you down." Sid shook it.

Then he helped Paul reassemble his clutch. Once everything was patched up, the two new friends—the new team—packed up and left together.

The next week, Paul and Sid returned to the Suffolk raceway, and Paul got in a run on the Rapide of 12.1 seconds at 117 mph. With that they eclipsed the previous track record of 12.2 held by none other than Gerald Givens on his Triumph. Sid was feeling good about his new plan.

Then at lunchtime the following Wednesday, Paul pulled up in front of Joe's. Sid told his father firmly that he was off to eat with his friend. Joe was angry but saw that this time there was no stopping Sid. The two men pulled away on their machines and raced over to GG's shop. There at the curb they sat, Sid astride the Rapide and Paul on the Gold Star, both revving their motors until GG walked outside. This time all Sid needed to do was point.

GG knew full well what it meant: countless guys had pulled up and issued such a challenge. Sid wanted GG to head out to "the old grain road." GG nodded and held up his keys, the signal that he would lock up and meet them.

While GG walked back inside to get ready, Sid and Paul rode off. When they arrived at the appointed spot, Paul decided to get in a practice run before GG arrived. On this trial run, Paul missed his shift from second to third, and the motor bellowed in protest. With only its front cylinder firing, the once proud Rapide returned, inching gingerly along. Sid knew the motor had just suffered serious damage.

Just then the sound of twin wailing megaphones announced GG's arrival. Working on instinct and nervous desperation, Sid checked the valves of the Rapide and found that the rear cylinder inlet was tight. He could picture in his mind what had happened: valve float from the over-revving had caused the collar to be knocked up off its normal seating, thus preventing the closure of the valve. And without closed valves, the motor loses compression and will not fire—and that is why the bike had limped back on only its front jug. Sid quickly slacked off the adjustor, and the valve returned to its seat. With the valve reset, he reinstalled the cap and, with one kick, had her rumbling on both pots again. It was a small miracle.

Their racing spot—the old grain road—was not far from the main gate of the Norfolk navy base, and the unmuffled sounds of their two drag bikes quickly drew an audience. About a dozen bikers (most in uniform) stood around, transfixed by the tension of the scene. Sid knew full well that the Rapide's untrustworthy valve collar might cause another ugly defeat and possibly even major motor damage. But now there was no backing down. GG and Sid hastily agreed to three runs.

The two riders, Paul and GG, lined up. GG's Triumph vertical twin alternately split the air with the wild shriek of ripping canvas, then a moan, as the motor backed down between blips of the throttle. Meanwhile the wicked snarl of the Vincent lifted the hair on Sid's neck.

Only then did it become apparent that the race was in need of a starter. Sid looked around imploringly at the crowd, and in response a young sailor dismounted from his Harley, strode over, and then stood ramrod straight between the two bikes. He extended his arms and eyed both riders. A few moments later, he nodded once, then twice, and then dropped his arms. The run was on. The Triumph slewed about from side to side, its rear wheel spinning violently as it fought to stay with the Rapide, succeeding all the way through first gear. GG lost a few feet as the Vincent bit second. Paul executed the shift flawlessly, booting the bike nearly a length ahead. Try as it might, GG's vertical twin could not haul alongside before both riders had to shut down, leaving themselves precious little room to pull up before running out of road.

Sid, one; GG, zero.

The Triumph was first back to the start line, its motor wailing down through each ratio, its rider now clenching his teeth, grim with determination. In sharp contrast, the Rapide limped back on one cylinder, the rear jug having died again. Sid launched into another quick repair, his hands working to the rapid, impatient beat of GG's waiting bike. GG looked confident, especially after seeing the Rap's post-run failure. Sid started the bike again, satisfied to hear it firing on both cylinders.

Once again the bikes stood paired at the line, ripping through the quiet of the afternoon with wails and snarls, their riders' eyes riveted on the starter, waiting for his arms to fall. They dropped again to the cry of spinning rear wheels, the acrid odor of burnt rubber and exhaust fumes. The two machines hurled off the mark, both clutches biting in unison. It was clear that though GG used all the rpm, horsepower, and torque his twisting, bucking Triumph could muster, it was to be of no avail. The Vincent launched straighter, with barely any wheel spin, and the crowd watched in awe as it widened the distance. As Sid listened to the cheering crowd, he realized that the onlookers were all rooting for him. The town bully was getting taken down and they loved it. Each successive gearshift and clutch engagement kicked the Vincent farther forward and away, decisively taking the second run.

As before, the Rapide returned firing on only one cylinder. The result induced a slight shudder into the bike's motion as Paul came to a stop. Once again Sid knew he would have to fix that same problem. Twice already he had sent the bike back to the line, and both times it had returned without suffering catastrophic internal damage. Sid knew the third run might be fatal. Wasn't he tempting fate at this point?

As Sid hesitated, GG killed his motor and edged his bike closer to the Rapide.

And then GG saw it.

That morning, Sid had painted a Star of David on his bike's rear fender. GG's face reddened to a deeper shade. "I ain't got all day," he barked.

"Give me a minute," Sid said, smiling.

GG grunted and restaged for the final run. Then he started his bike and waited at the line, brutally whipping the throttle as if he were cracking a whip. Sid knelt and mutely administered the needed dose of spanner work.

Before the final thunderous instant carved two burnt lines upon the tarmac, Sid examined GG: he was sweaty and looked somehow smaller, public failure a new experience for him. It was clear that he was praying for a mechanical failure, or some other miracle, to declare him the winner. Sid humbly prayed for his motor to hold its guts together once more. He cautioned Paul to hold down the rpm and out-torque GG as he had done before. Both machines, stinking hot and oil stained from the high revs and wide-open throttles, sat at the line momentarily hushed by their riders.

After a last glance around, the racers lined up straight and true. The flagman walked again to his place down the road. His arms fell, and GG's vertical twin ran up full and wailed a single note. GG, throwing all caution to the wind, wound the poor mill to its absolute limit. Paul held the Vincent to just under 5,000 rpm and launched himself on a rising throttle. GG swerved from side to side as his clutch bit, and for a moment, it seemed he would collide with the Rapide. But he regained control and the run was on. Thrashed to its limit, the Triumph responded valiantly and leapt out to lead the Rapide. But it didn't last. An instant later Paul roared past. Sid's strategy had worked perfectly. The big twin could not be bested.

In the end, Paul had cut three flawless runs without missing a single shift. For Sid the elation was overwhelming. He listened to the sounds of his Rapide's return, and this time it was firing on both cylinders, as if in the prime of life.

Sid walked over to Paul and slapped him on the back as he killed the motor. The silence was dramatic. GG looked at the crowd of riders and saw them smiling at his defeat.

Stepping forward from out of the tight circle that had closed around the two bikes, Sid stood before GG and delivered the line he'd rehearsed in his head, night after night as he worked in the garage: "Hey, Gerald, take that goddamn thing home and don't bring it back until it can pull the slack out of the rear chain." And he slapped him hard on the shoulder.

"I'll be back," Gerald vowed, but his voice broke as he said it.

Gerald Givens sold that bike the next week and never built another to take its place.

* * *

A Score to Settle

In the days that followed, Sid would sit in his garage, studying his Rapide and dreaming of the day he would take her to Bonneville for a crack at besting Rollie Free. Free had seized the record back in 1948 with a run of 150 and then later raised that mark to 163-plus on a factory-built Lightning. Sid believed he had built a machine capable of seizing that record. One day he would make the trip and prove it.

But in his dreams he was already there.

Part Two

Sid's Kid

When it comes to machinery,
all men are not created equal.

—Phil Irving

Chapter Four

Why God Made Sunday

One night, when I was five years old, I woke to voices, laughter. I climbed out of bed, crept down the hallway, and snuck into the den. There I saw my dad giving a slideshow. Up on the screen flashed a red motorcycle. Some of the men watching I already knew—a guy named Mac, another named Paul—but the rest were strangers.

After a while, I spotted something in the room's darkness I hadn't seen before. To the side of the screen, I could make out a square of red fabric with white piping on the edges. The tough canvas was folded and draped over a chair to show off a drawing in a painted circle of white.

Suddenly, I wanted just one thing: a good look at that drawing. Knowing I would be spotted, I ran toward it quickly. As I got closer, I could make out a crazed, rail-thin rider holding the front wheel of a bike with his hands, as he powered along on roller skates. A can trailed behind like a kite hooked to the motor he had strapped to his chest. The can was emblazoned with a skull and crossbones. It was the coolest thing I had ever seen, and I couldn't believe it was in my hands.

Just then Sid saw me. He walked over and patted my head.

"What is it, Daddy?" I asked, my hand tracing the lines on the painted canvas.

He explained that it was his old racing cover. In the pits, he would drape it over the Rattler—as the red Rapide came to be known—between runs or if it rained. Just then my mother rushed in, lifted me up, and carried me back to bed, but not before I heard Sid brag that in its final form, the Rattler was never beaten, not even by cars.

From that night on, I pretended to ride motorcycles whenever I played. In the den, my toys included a box of disassembled racing trophies. They were Sid's version of Lincoln Logs: granite pieces, large wooden bases, long columns with screw holes. Some were chrome; some were painted gold or black and white. The pieces came from the many large, multilayered trophies he had won while drag racing. The nicest of the small ones he kept on top of an old dresser out in the garage, but I played with the rest. Sid loved watching me build towers with them, but if I ever followed him out to the garage where the real motorcycle sat parked, he would pick me up and hand me over to my mother.

At that age, I loved to wander all over our house, but what interested me most was the attached garage where my father kept an immaculate standard Vincent Black Shadow. I loved to sit on it and play with the handlebar controls. It was a special object, *the* treasure within the house.

But things changed that night when I saw the racing cover. Now the black motorcycle in the garage seemed drained of power. It just couldn't compete in my imagination with the mythic red motorcycle I had seen up on the screen.

"Daddy?" I asked. "What happened to the Rattler?"

He told me then that he had swapped it for the black bike right before I was born.

"You see, I'm your dad now," he insisted. "I don't need to be out drag racing."

Hearing him say it, I was heartbroken.

The man I knew had given up his Bonneville dream. What he did now was run Joe's Meat Market. He had bought the store from his father on a strict payment schedule. Once my father married, making those payments became a great struggle, and the mounting debt possessed incredible psychic weight. At times it threatened to burst our house.

When Sid met my mother, she was a young, attractive widow with three small children—two girls, Linda and Robin, and one boy, David, who was the oldest. I was much younger than them, but we lived together until each in turn went away to college.

I don't remember much happiness between my parents, only the intense pressure to secure more money. I noticed it most acutely at night. Because my father's shop required electricity to keep the meat from going bad, power outages were nail-biting events.

I recall waking up one night in the middle of a storm; a lightning strike had taken out the power. I stayed in bed, watching the candle-light flicker. I listened to my parents' nervous conversation. My father pacing, wondering what he should do. My mother telling Sid to stay put, that he could do nothing. Eventually, though, Sid couldn't take the worry. Then I heard the front door close.

After he left, I could hear my mother talking to herself. She was arguing with God, asking again why he had to take her beloved first husband, Morris. She begged for the strength to survive, but then broke down and cried until my sisters roused themselves to sit with her.

Despite all the problems, I loved my father's meat market. It was a true corner shop with one long glass counter where meats were displayed. I loved its order: the slicers and the register and the large flat wooden cutting blocks sitting neatly on the back counter. Everything was clean and gleaming, especially the array of long knives with their glossy black handles. My favorite thing in the place was the walk-in cooler, which you entered via a large door at the far end of the counter.

Inside, massive sides of beef hung on big hooks in the cold, quiet air. The red meat and white fat blended together, a vision as mesmerizing as any abstract painting. On hot summer days, I used to play alone inside the cooler, moving carefully between the walls and the hanging slabs of meat.

Joe had done well for himself with this store, but by the time Sid took over the neighborhood around it had begun to deteriorate. I was just a young child, and at first I didn't understand what was happening to our family business. I thought food stamps were a step up from money: they were so much more colorful and came in books. With my mom's permission, I had often walked home with some of our best customers in order to play with their kids. I thought then that the nearby housing projects, with their big common yards, were the coolest places ever invented for playing tag.

But by the time I was seven and starting second grade, I had begun to fear the changes in the world around our store. When Sid locked up and took me home, I would cover my ears as I watched him tap the glass to test the horn of his newly installed burglar-alarm system. Then came the night when Sid arrived home and told my mother he had just been robbed at knifepoint. He was still shaking and his skin had an ashen color.

After that I was forbidden from spending time at the store. Then the battle over the garage became even more intense. When Sid came home, he liked going out to spend time alone with his Vincent. Eventually, I would go after him. I would open the door and quietly slip in. Creep to the work bench. Climb up on Sid's stool in order to grab tools—a hammer or a wrench. At the sight, Sid would shout, "Don't!" And if that wasn't enough to stop me, he would call for my mother. Here they were in agreement: I was too young to be out in the garage.

It's not that he didn't want to spend time with me. He loved taking me for rides and from the beginning I loved riding. By the time I was five, I was going for short rides with him around the neighborhood. I hugged that big black Vincent and loved feeling the motor's rumble up through the tank and into my chest. At age seven, I was big enough to sit behind him in the proper "two-up" position.

By the time of the robbery, it was clear that the store was going under. Even worse, simply working there had become a terrifying prospect. Sid was paralyzed. The more my mother begged him to act, the more he hesitated. They would fight, and then I would hear only her voice. I knew the silence meant he was dressing. I would slip out of bed and dress too. Then Sid would open my bedroom door and peer in.

"I'm going for a ride. Do you want to come with me?"

* * *

We would leave in the early morning light of a Sunday and head deep into the countryside. The bruised black sky fading into the blue of morning, the burly bark of the exhaust, the smell of the oil on my hands—all of it soothed me.

On those rides, Sid almost always headed south into North Carolina. I suppose he was retracing the roads he first discovered when, as a young hot shoe, he had dreams of seeing off all comers at Daytona Beach. Usually we headed out to Nags Head, often paralleling the inland coastal waterway. There were ferries and seafood restaurants. It was the perfect route for a bike: no interstates, little traffic, and plenty of places to stop by the side of the road for a stretch and a few pictures.

For lunch Sid always selected a restaurant that faced the sea and had a seat where you could keep one eye on your bike while you ate. I'm sure plenty of people know a place like this: the thick wooden tables next to the large windows with the blinds open so you can stare out at the sea and its whitecaps, the iced tea in smoked glasses, the menus in plastic. Sand in the carpet and the sounds of seagulls just off shore. Often we'd talk to strangers who were curious: what kind of motorcycle is that anyway? Sid never tired of talking about Vincents. As he liked to say back then, "Isn't this why God made Sunday?"

Chapter Five

Near Miss

Till I was about seven, we rode only the Black Shadow, virtually every Sunday. It was our ritual, our way of dealing with the stresses at home and at the meat market. Then in 1973, two decades after Sid became smitten with the Vincent, he encountered his first Ducati V-twin, an unsold 1972 gold GT model, gathering dust in a local Norfolk dealership. The store was in the same building that had once housed GG's Indian shop, but Sid didn't hold that against this new machine. Most evenings, he would close up Joe's Meat Market and drive over to look in from the street at this new big twin sitting on a box, high above the rest of the dealer's offerings: somber Norton twins, plus a few Ducati singles. Sid had admired Ducatis for years but had never owned one—the singles were just too small. But this Ducati—their first big twin—entranced him. Ducatis do that: they seduce.

It is hard to imagine now, but Ducati began, not as a maker of motorcycles, but as a tech firm that sold sophisticated radios and transmitting devices. This work came to an end during World War II, when Allied bombs effectively destroyed the Ducati factory in Bologna. After war's end, Ducati entered the business of making internal combustion motors suitable for use in mopeds, vehicles the Italian government deemed essential for its national economic-recovery plan. Without transport, you can't move a workforce, and postwar Italy embraced the scooter as the ideal vehicle.

By late 1946, Ducati was in the motorcycle business. The first bikes were just push-pedal affairs but they bore all the spirit of Italy: flair, beauty, and speed. Engineer Aldo Farinelli, the man behind these first machines, must have seen his share of Whizzers, or their European equivalents. For Farinelli's motor, a 48 cc two-speed four-stroke, affectionately dubbed Cucciolo (the puppy) remains a very impressive design, complete with "pull rod" operated overhead valves. The motor is also placed at the base of the frame, so the bike possesses a low center of gravity, a characteristic critical to good handling.

In 1954 engineer Fabio Taglioni, the famous Dr. T, came to work for Ducati. His first effort, the 100 cc Gran Sport, inaugurated the line of Ducati singles that continued uninterrupted until the appearance of the GT twin. Shortly after the Gran Sport's introduction, Taglioni discovered that his powerful, high-revving motor suffered from valve-spring breakage. His solution was to eliminate the springs and use another cam to close the valves. This arrangement, called "desmodromic," remains Ducati's signature. Taglioni's daring in engineering was matched by his eye for beauty. Those early Ducati singles (with their jelly-mold gas tanks) have stunningly sexy lines.

Later Taglioni drew up a twin. The result, the GT, was a true benchmark. When in 1972 Paul Smart won the first Imola 200 on a 750 SS, his thrilling victory surprised everyone, including Ducati. It was the turning point that led to the company's current dominance on the racetrack and to its bikes' enduring appeal.

Sid's lust for the gold Duke in that shop eventually drove him to sell some spare parts and buy it. From the very first start, Sid relished its rich, booming exhaust. Yet that rumble did not translate into a rough ride. The chassis damped out vibration and enabled effortless cruising. Sid especially loved how he could practically lounge astride the long, lanky bike.

Soon he was out in the countryside, marveling at the GT's ability to sweep through turns and eat up road. Ever since, Sid has been as much a Ducati fan as a lover of Vincents. The Vincent was still faster and pulled harder, but it was cramped and it vibrated more.

From the moment I saw the Duke, I loved this new toy, with its bright paint scheme. Unlike the Shadow, it had big round foot pegs that were much more inviting, and its seat was thick and plush. The sound of the engine was higher in pitch and sharper. The way it moved was also different, with much less flexing in the chassis. But when my dad gave it the gas, even I could tell that it was not the equal of his Vincent. Still, it was a great ride.

My mother, however, did not share our excitement. Now their fights had a new topic: the Ducati. Didn't he realize what was happening down at the store? He was going bankrupt. What right did he have to buy himself a new toy? Didn't he understand that we were about to end up on the street?

After a few weeks of this, Sid sold the Ducati. I remember going out to the garage and staring mournfully at the empty space. Worse, I worried this loss was one of many yet to come.

But shortly after he sold the Ducati, an opportunity came Sid's way. The other tenant of the building that housed the meat market was a savings and loan, and it wanted to buy Sid out. The offer would allow Sid to pay off his father and have enough cash left over to follow his dream and open up his own motorcycle shop. For the first time in my memory, the mood in our house was bright and optimistic.

The first Big Sid's was located on a side street called Sunnyside Drive. It was hardly the ideal location, but Sid was convinced his clients would be willing to seek him out. And the rent was cheap.

From the beginning, things were different for me in that store. In the meat market, I had been free to explore. The meat slicers and power saws were off-limits but that was about it. In the motorcycle shop, however, I always sensed that my father's eyes were on me, fearful that I might knock into something and send a bike crashing down. I was now eight years old, and I thought I was finally ready to use the tools. Sid, however, did not agree.

He knew I was old enough to handle basic tasks such as using a screwdriver or tightening a bolt, but even then I always felt his anxiety when I picked up these simple tools. It was as if he knew I would fail and he couldn't resist correcting me. When I started to turn the screw or bolt the wrong way, he would never just let me make the mistake and learn on my own. Instead he always stopped me, with a lecture, no matter how inconsequential the mistake.

His attitude to the young boys who were his customers was different. One day a boy a couple of years older than me pulled up on a beat-up moped. He burst into the store and explained through his tears that he had just crashed and the handlebars were now bent. He told Sid that his father was going to whip his ass. My dad and the boy stepped outside. Sid straddled the bike, looked down at the badly twisted bars, and with one clean jerk returned them to straight. The boy was suddenly beaming. I watched Sid put his arm around him. I could tell that my father admired that boy's brashness.

But despite Sid's magical ways with bikes, by that first winter he knew he had a problem. If you are a man like Big Sid, you think about motorcycles every waking moment of every day, all year round. Even in winter there is plenty of maintenance to be done. But this was not the case for the casual riders who were Sid's typical customers. As the weather got colder, they disappeared. Sid got a rude awakening, and so did the whole family. As Sid said, "You can't eat chrome."

The days wore on into January and then February, and a deep cold settled into the house. It reminded me of the cooler at Joe's. The bathroom was the worst, especially in the morning, when I had to shower before school. I had to think carefully about how to dress to stay warm in my own house. And my mother—who had spent my whole life cursing Joe's Meat Market—began to lament the absence of the food Sid once regularly brought home.

Things then went from bad to very bad. One afternoon, Sid was trying to fit a freshly rebuilt Honda 750 motor back into its frame. He shifted it one way, and then another, and then he felt a sudden and intense pressure followed by so much pain that he simply dropped the motor and fell to the floor. Sid had crushed a disk in his back.

A long hospital stay followed, punctuated by surgery. Our visits to the hospital were sobering. The one thing I thought of as a constant was my father's strength. I had seen him do things mere mortals couldn't do. Sitting next to him in the hospital, I saw a very different Sid, flat on his back and wincing in agony.

I couldn't believe that this was the same man who used to walk around the shop with a moped tucked under each arm like a couple loaves of bread. He used to sling complete two-hundred-pound motors around from the workbench to the assembly bench without assistance, acts that astonished not just me but his mechanics.

But he'd had plenty of accidents too. The time he hit the police chief's wife in her sedan. The time he rear-ended a Chevy and got nailed from behind by Bugs on his Shadow. The time he had stupidly tried to oil the Matchless's rear chain with the bike running and it snatched a finger and lopped off the tip.

But this time, when my father finally returned to the shop, he wasn't the same. He was disgusted with himself and, for the first time, with motorcycles. Now when I heard my parents talk about their problems late at night, Sid said things I'd never heard him say before. Motorcycles were a waste of time. You can't make a living out of a hobby. It was best to simply liquidate and get out.

I came home from school one Friday afternoon, and while I ate at one end of the table, my mother sat quietly at the other and patiently filled out paperwork to get the benefits Sid was entitled to as a vet. Then she filled out an application for admission into a local engineering program. After dinner I retreated to my room to do my homework. While I sat at my desk with my books open before me, I could hear my parents talk about my mother's idea. As I listened, I learned that my father had once dreamed of going to college and becoming an engineer.

This effort on my mother's part was a special act. And Sid was moved by it but told her firmly no. He had to make a living now and motorcycles were all he knew.

At first my mom resisted and said he was selling himself short; he may not have done well in high school but he was smart and he had a gift. He understood how to fix things.

"No," Sid simply said. And then, "I'll do better. I'll find a better place."

Inspired by my mother, Sid broke the lease and got out while there was still enough money for one more shot. It was that or risk losing the house.

Over the next few days, he began searching and found a better location, right on Virginia Beach Boulevard, a major urban artery. After the move, business picked up, and the location did help, but the biggest boost came as a result of the 1973 OPEC oil embargo. Suddenly, more economical forms of transportation were in demand, and bike sales took off. For the first time since Sid's youth, motorized bicycles came back into vogue in the States. He took on two lines of mopeds— Cimatti, an Italian brand, and the Austrian-made Puch. Soon he was selling several on a good day. Suddenly, we had some money, and Sid began to believe in motorcycling again.

One afternoon, while Sid was stopped at a gas station, he spotted the gutted remains of a motorcycle tucked away in a corner. It was covered in rust with only a few small spots of red and black paint on the tank. He looked harder and realized it was a beat-up Ducati 750 GT, or it had once been one. The owner of the gas station had taken it in exchange for some car parts from a sailor who had left it to rot under a pier. Sid offered seventy-five dollars for it, peeling off three twenties and promising the last fifteen when he received the title (which Sid never got).

The rebuild of that Ducati is the first ground-up restoration job I remember clearly. When Sid initially showed me the bike, I was doubtful that even he could bring such an abused pile of parts back to life. Over the next several Saturdays, I would come into the shop and watch him sitting on his stool contemplating that husk of a machine. The engine looked like a weathered coral formation. Its cylinder fins and covers had the pronounced mottling that salt air leaves on metal. The tires broke to pieces as Sid removed them from the wheels.

Soon the Duke's lump of a motor was gone, off to a buddy Sid called by the oddly collective name the Midnight Crew. The Crew was another Vincent owner, and general all-around bike nut. At that time, he was working the parts counter in a Yamaha shop while doing engine work out of his home on the side.

The Crew's Rapide was also from that small batch of red ones Philip Vincent told Sid about during his Stevenage visit. That particular Vincent had arrived in Norfolk while Sid was away in the army. Willie Wooten, who along with Johnny Marshall, had entered into that New Year's Eve bet with Sid, had tracked it down in California. After flying out, Willie rode it all the way back. Many Tidewater bikers later heard him recount the tale.

Eventually, Wooten sold it to the Crew, a man who to this day is my father's most trusted machine guy. When the Crew sets up a bike, it is virtually flawless and runs like a top.

While the Crew was "breathing upon" the motor—to use one of Sid's expressions—Sid began building up the chassis. When I visited the shop, I would admire the various components spread out in preparation for final assembly. It was exciting to watch the project come together and I wanted to help.

Almost every week, my mother dropped me off at the shop after taking me to Sabbath services. During those visits, I watched the Duke come together. Then one afternoon I came in and the chassis was fully assembled. Sid was busy fitting the seat and tank. At that point, the tank was only a primed rust red and the seat was just a bare base topped by a loose foam lump.

With everything in position, Sid pulled over his stool. He sat and stared. Then he picked up a clipboard and a pencil. He said, "I am thinking about the paint scheme and the shape I want to give the seat." He showed me how he saw a gentle step-up in the middle to distinguish the rear passenger's perch. He explained that one thing he hated about the Duke was the line of the seat—it was just a flat slab.

Then we turned to the tank, and for the first time I began to discern all its less obvious geometric shapes and angles. You had to be able to spot those inner patterns, Sid explained, if you were going to get it pinstriped. That was the trick of custom painting.

I sat with my own sheet and drew, and for the first time, we worked together in the back of the shop.

Sid looked over at what I was doing and smiled. As we sketched, he told me he thought the broad two-tone paint scheme the Italians favored was garish. And he was right too. The broad stripes actually hide the graceful shape Taglioni gave his tank. That afternoon Sid settled on a restrained silver gray with elegant crème and black piping, a combination I have loved ever since.

Soon the motor was back from the Crew. I couldn't believe the transformation. The water marks had vanished. The side covers and caps gleamed. The cylinders and fins were a beautiful uniform gray. The metal was so clean you could study the surface and see its pores. It even smelled clean.

By the following Sunday, the Duke was ready for her maiden

voyage. I held open the door while my father walked the silver Duke outside, and as he rocked it back on its center stand, he said out loud that it was so easy a child could do it.

"Can I try?" I said.

Sid frowned. After some thought, he rocked it back off the stand and demonstrated how to do it. Then he walked around to the other side of the bike. "Go ahead," he said.

I grabbed the bars and rocked the bike forward. The bike was now free in my hands and, feeling its full weight, I let it bobble slightly, first toward me, then away. If Sid hadn't been on the other side, the Duke would have fallen over, but he wasn't angry. "When you are a little older," he said, "you'll be able to reach the far end of the handlebar better."

I stepped back, still clammy from the near disaster, zipped up my jacket, and put on my helmet. Sid started the bike, and off we went, heading south toward Nags Head. Sid sang to himself as we rode, and once we were out in the country, he began rolling open the throttle.

"Feel that!" he yelled into my ear. "When it comes onto the cam, it really moves."

"Yeah!" I shouted back. I had no idea what he meant, but we sure were going fast. "So much better than the gold one. The Crew sure can build 'em."

But my father had something else on his mind. "I wonder—the Vin and the Duke? Which would walk off from the other? When you're older, we'll find out."

By the time moped sales dried up in the late 1970s, Sid had managed to build a steady base of customers comprised mostly of hard riders, loners. These were guys who could do the job themselves but now trusted Sid, not only to get their bikes running, but also set them up right. Sid called this "fettling"—hearing in the sounds of the motor what was needed for optimum running and making the slightest of adjustments to get it there. Nothing made Sid happier.

And it brought him a certain kind of fame. He was becoming a name known to hard-core bikers, where tuning commands deep respect. But my mother still had to work, from 1974 on, down at the Norfolk navy base, as a clerk in the civil service. I endured her spite toward Sid because I understood it: she never recovered from nursing her first husband through his painful death from colon cancer. Just as important, I never doubted her love for me. Once her older kids were out of the house, I was the only thing that kept her going.

She always believed that she would not have had to work if Sid had not turned away customers whose bikes weren't worth repairing. He often did this. But sometimes I agreed with Sid. Some jobs were a waste of everyone's time and resources.

Obvious examples were the cheap mopeds that flooded the market at the end of the moped boom. Crude models sold in stores like Sears and Montgomery Ward. Sid turned down a service contract from an outfit that rented to tourists at Virginia Beach. That happened right before my mother went back to work. She was angry about it for years. But I could see Sid's point: those bikes really were shit—all they did was break. On the other hand, my mother had a point. Often if Sid saw the job as beneath him, he would shame the owner into doing it on his own. In his eyes, he was being a mentor—but this sort of thing drove my mother crazy.

My school was only a short walk from our house. I left in the morning with a key to the front door. When I came home, I had the TV to keep me company, and my books. I used the new microwave when I got hungry. All those long motorcycle rides with my father had forced me to develop my imagination. I enjoyed having the house to myself, and I sat at the dining room table most afternoons and read.

Having to work did little to brighten my mother's mood. Now when she came home she was too tired to pick a fight with my father. Instead she fixed herself something light to eat and lay on the couch watching TV. A few hours later, Sid would come home, usually after stopping to pick up a burger.

Gradually, an equilibrium settled in the house as my parents' relationship limped along. It was far from an ideal situation but it wasn't so bad for me. I stopped worrying about living on the street and concentrated on school and being a kid.

My mother sought what little comfort she could in her faith, so Saturdays were usually okay. She and I would drive down to B'nai Israel, where she would sit with the women and I would sit with the men. We attended the orthodox congregation out of loyalty to her first husband, who had been an observant Jew. He had taught my mother how to keep a kosher house and how to say the prayers Jewish women say.

But Sundays were different. My mother had nowhere to go, and all the bitterness inevitably came pouring out. She was mad as hell at having to work, and she let Sid know it. Eventually, he would flee the house, usually with me in tow.

Most weekends, if the weather was good, we would drive to the shop and then roll out either the Ducati or the Vincent. Sid didn't consider it a ride if we didn't do at least a hundred miles, and often we did much more.

* * *

On a Sunday in the fall, my father and I were out for our usual trip. The leaves were turning, falling from the canopy as we sped along. I felt them brush my helmet before they flew behind us into the bike's churning wake. I sat gripping his belt and fell asleep, lulled by the pleasant sensation of the ride. Then I felt his hand hooked behind me. He did that often. My eyes fluttered open.

The next instant we sped past a bronze WPA marker commemorating a Civil War retreat route. Sid turned to me and said, "Did you see that?"

I didn't respond because I could see straight ahead an abandoned car lying clear across the entire road. In that instant I knew we were going to crash. I was nine years old. I was going to die.

Seeing the fear in my eyes, Sid whipped his head back around. At that moment, the car was perhaps a hundred feet ahead and our speed was about 75 mph. We were about to hit hard. Sid slammed the brakes full on while angling toward the right shoulder.

I braced for impact. The Duke shimmied as its tires began to skid and then skip. I rode up on the seat and was pinned against Sid's back. With each shudder our helmets smacked together and I felt my body jerked hard this way and then that. Each jolt terrified me. I saw us going right into the car. Several times I had heard Sid tell the story of the unfortunate Vincent factory tester who broadsided a double-decker bus. The punch line was that they found his head on the roof.

Just before impact, Sid cranked the handlebar right and locked the front wheel. In the next instant, the entire bike pivoted sideways as the still-turning rear wheel began to catapult forward. It was an improvement. I felt relief in knowing that I would hit the ground first.

Everything happened in slow motion. With the Duke now roughly parallel to the car, I sensed the wheels were losing contact with the road. I was certain what would happen next: the bike would hit the ground and then we would slide into the car. I looked down at the seductive gray blur of road, so like ocean water. I imagined us separating from the bike and a crazy Evel Knievel tumble clear of the collision.

By laying the bike near flat over onto its right side, Sid managed to clear the car's front bumper. Then he stomped the ground with his right foot, and the Duke popped back up. Still in control, Sid sliced sharply off the road. Now we raced across a small stretch of grass straight toward a line of trees. While continuing to break furiously, Sid fought the Duke through a series of sharp wobbles as the handlebars slammed left and then right, slapping either side of the tank. It felt as if I was on a pogo stick. Then just as suddenly we came to a halt with Sid's legs spread on either side of the bike. He collapsed forward and lay on the tank with his hands lying limply on the bars.

I listened to him rapidly suck air in gasps. Then as he quieted, I crumbled off the seat. Everything inside me had let go. When my foot touched the ground, I couldn't stand but collapsed in a heap.

Sid continued to straddle the bike. Finally, he sat upright, took off his helmet, and let it fall to rest right-side up in the grass. He managed to kick out the side stand and dismount. His face was covered in sweat and his body was still tensed as if ready to land another blow with his fist.

"You okay?" he asked.

"Yeah."

We both stared at the trees and together realized that we were not far from where the embankment fell off to a small stream. He began to pace, and at first I feared he had broken his ankle. The side of his right boot has heavily scarred. He took a step. "The soul is singed," he said with a laugh. Eventually, he stopped at the edge and stared down at the yellowish green water.

I got up and joined him. We were still alive. I looked down at my hands and the palms and fingers were stained with faint black streaks from where I had clutched Sid's leather belt.

I heard him say, "Don't tell your mother."

"No," I answered. "Of course not." Looking at the stand of trees on the far side of the water, I began to relax. What Sid had done was superhuman. He had saved my life.

"She'll never let you ride again."

Even then the thought was unbearable. "We can't tell anybody," I said.

Sid nodded.

That evening over dinner my mother said, "So, did you boys enjoy your ride?"

Sid looked at me, and I looked at him.

Then I said, "Sure. It was fun."

If I was old enough not to tell my mother, Sid knew it was time, and so from this, our brush with death, came a great thing—a new Honda XR75 dirt bike.

Sid loved to tell that part of the story: how he rolled it out with a flourish and the pure joy on my face. I ran over to sit on its black seat, eager to learn if my arms were long enough to grab the bright red grips on the handlebar. Then I stood up to see if I was tall enough to straddle it and—yes!—put both feet on the ground.

One by one I met all my father's conditions. Only then would he show me how to kick-start the bike. I got the hang of that procedure quickly and began to think that learning to ride was going to be a piece of cake. I'd just teach myself and skip Sid's lectures. A few minutes later, I pulled off, promptly rolled the throttle wide open, and shot straight toward the brick wall that was the back of the house. Not knowing what to do, I simply dropped the bike and slid, coming to a halt a few feet from contact. I popped up, sobered, and now willing to listen to my father, but my enthusiasm was as strong as ever.

After a few more lessons, I was flying around the backyard, madly in love with the combination of risk and control that riding a bike provides. It was only a little dirt bike, not even legal to ride on the streets, but to me, back then, that Honda was all a boy could wish for. From fourth grade on, I came home alone, rolled out my Honda, and rode my ass off until my mom came home from work.

I did doughnuts and wheelies, but my favorite thing was to ride flat out straight toward the chain fence and then drop the bike into a slide, repeating what I did the very first time I got on the bike but now in a controlled way. I loved it when the bike's wheels came to rest against the metal grid of the fence. Many times I would lie there and take in the experience, not moving until I felt the heat from the exhaust pipe burning through my jeans.

On Sundays I would beg my father to take me to the local dirt parks, where I could really manhandle my Honda through the mud. But once we got back to Big Sid's to put the bike away, the fights would start, usually because he didn't want me to tinker with it.

The first thing Sid likes to do when servicing a motorcycle is check the plugs. They're the first significant bolt on any engine. Any tuner worth his salt can read spark-plug color: black and oily, black and sooty, shades of brown, off-whites, grays—each shade a different meaning. Generally, the darker the color the richer the fuel mixture—which means too much gas is being introduced into the motor's intake of oxygen. In addition to color, the texture of the buildup around the plug's center electrode reflects the amount of oil present, as well as the intensity of the combustion, in the chamber. On this particular afternoon, I wanted to see for myself, so I went for the spark-plug wrench. Sid must have been feeling generous, because for once he didn't stop me.

He only said, "Remember, unscrew. If you go the wrong way on a spark plug you can strip out the head."

I could hear in his voice that he sensed disaster in the offing, and it hurt. Angry, I went ahead and pulled off the black spark-plug cap, slid the wrench on to the plug, and promptly turned it the wrong way. Sid exploded, "Stop! Jesus Christ! You'll ruin the motor."

"I am going the right way," I said, reversing direction.

"How could you be so stupid? Well, that's what I get for letting a kid do a man's job."

I was nine. I wore a watch, so I knew how a dial hand moved, but when it came to working with tools, I just couldn't get it down. Finally, the plug came out, and I handed it to Sid. He looked to see if there was metal in the threads: luckily there was none. That meant the mating threads were still intact in the cylinder's head. Sid had yelled at me to stop just in time. When he realized the bike was going to be okay, he tried to apologize for his outburst, but I was already too hurt to care. I ran out of the store to be alone in the back lot. It faced trees and had rocks strewn on its unpaved chalky surface. I picked up the rocks and hurled them into the dark grass, screaming curses loud enough for my father to hear.

After my first effort, any time I tried to pick up a tool and do the work Sid would stop me. Before I had always accepted it, but when he gave me the Honda, I changed. It was my bike. I wanted to work on it no matter what he thought. The most painful thing was that I always felt deep down that he was right to stop me—I secretly feared that I'd make a critical mistake. Teaching me how to work on motorcycles was what he wanted to do, a way to really connect, and yet we could never manage it. I knew I didn't have his gift. And he knew it too, and that's why I hated him. Neither of us said it directly but it didn't matter. For the next few years, the only time we bonded was when we were out on the road, riding together, but we said little then, lost in our own thoughts and the blur of what was passing us by.

Chapter Six

Another Jewish Faulkner

When I turned sixteen, I got my driver's license. I could legally drive a car, but what I really wanted to do was ride a motorcycle on the street. Sid was sympathetic, and I was too old for my mother to stop me. But Sid didn't want me learning on just any old bike.

On our way home from a trip visiting relatives in Baltimore, Sid spotted a Matchless Super Clubman twin propped against a light pole by the side of the road, with a FOR SALE sign taped to its headlamp. It looked just like his first road bike, right down to the orangish red paint. We pulled over and, while my mom and I sat in the van, he bought the machine on the spot.

Sid spent the next few weeks passionately sorting out the Matchless. The very sight of it took him back to his own first days up on two wheels. It wasn't a Vincent, of course, but how he had loved his Clubman until his Rapide had come along. After kicking this one to life, he rode off smiling. When he returned, he looked disappointed. It just didn't have the get-up-and-go of the original. Sid's had been a 1949 model, while this one was from 1952.

The dramatic difference in performance confirmed Sid's sense that as the tooling aged, the quality of the British bikes really had diminished. Even at the height of their success, the English factories were turning out parts on mills and lathes that dated back to the 1930s. As these machines wore out, the resulting engines suffered. Early Rapides, for example, were often faster than late Shadows. This deterioration was especially pronounced with the smaller English bikes. At the time, I listened to Sid's complaints, but they didn't mean much to me. As far as I was concerned, the fact that he didn't like the Matchless meant only that he should have no objections to me taking the bike.

I learned to ride it, on Sundays, in the empty parking lot of a nearby discount store. I was determined to learn fast because I had the fantasy of riding it to my high school. The thought of how cool that would be was more than enough incentive for me to put up with my father's terse instructions.

The biggest issue was the setup of the foot controls. On the little Honda I'd been riding, the rear brake pedal was on the right and the gearshift pedal was on the left. On the Matchless, it was the other way around. Additionally, the gearshift's pattern was different. As on most old British bikes, you selected first by hooking the gearshift up with your foot, then you engaged the other gears by depressing the lever. On most modern motorcycles, you enter first by depressing the lever, and then you slip your foot under the pedal and shift up for all higher gears. Sid had pointed out these differences to me many times on the Vincent, but now I had to perform the switch over.

And it was a crucial thing to learn. If you get it wrong, you can find yourself madly stomping on the gearshift lever in the vain hope that it will actuate the rear brake. Less problematic but more humiliating is when you attempt to pull away and think you are in first gear but you are really in second (because you shifted down and not up): then the bike lurches forward in one gangly heave and dies.

That first day, I did this often. Every time Sid would crack, "Your fire went out."

It was a point of pride with him that he rarely stalled a motorcycle and that a motorcycle he set up never stalled. It was always the rider's fault.

But the more Sid lectured me, the more mistakes I made. Now I felt ridiculous in the French sailor's shirt I had bought after I saw Jean-Luc Godard's *Breathless*. I had imagined myself pulling up in the high school parking lot, looking for all the world like a French Marlon Brando on my badass motorcycle. The only problem was that I couldn't even get the thing to go ten feet.

In disgust I put the bike on the rear stand and sat under a tree while Sid went off in the van to bring us back some burgers. With my father gone, I was finally alone with that Matchless. In those minutes, listening to her motor tink, she became my bike. I could smell the exhaust and the stinking-hot engine smattered with singed engine oil. Freed from the helmet, my head felt nearly as hot, my hair a tangled, sweat-drenched mop. I was abusing this delicate creature and exhausting myself in the process.

I got up and stroked the seat and worked the throttle some, while studying just how quickly the carburetor's slide responded. Sid always liked just a little slack in the throttle, to ensure that the cable at rest was not under tension. The trick to a clean start was a steady, progressive opening of the throttle.

Sid finally returned, and we ate a quick lunch. Soon after, I had the bike puttering along. That got Sid's approval.

"You are a quick study," he told me, as we rode home in the van.

I listened to the Matchless creak as it rocked. It felt good to hear him say so. I could settle down and get the hang of something. Now I was ready to make my dream come true: to ride the Matchless to school.

By then I had transferred to the Norfolk Academy, a ritzy private day school. It was the age of busing: many of the best kids had already left public school and I wanted to go too. My mother got me the necessary scholarship. She felt deep shame when pleading our case before the headmaster, but once again, her desire to give me a shot at a good life pushed her to her knees. After I transferred there, I became a good student, especially in English.

But Sid's answer to my request was always no. He was afraid that the bike would get knocked over in the high school parking lot. He had a low opinion of teenage drivers, especially when it came to parking. My inability to live out this fantasy didn't trouble me too much. Deep down I probably knew I wasn't ready. So I left the idea hanging and focused instead on college. My number one requirement was that the school be far away.

In the spring of 1984, as school wound down, my mom greeted me one afternoon with an opened acceptance letter. I was off to Dartmouth, and, perhaps best of all, thanks again to her endless form filling, I had won a Stoneman Scholarship that pretty much covered four years of tuition. I was finally going away, though without a motorcycle.

The next summer, I made it a point to go riding with my dad. With a year of college under my belt, I was determined to return to Dartmouth in the fall on a bike. Now no matter how late I stayed out with my friends on Saturday night, I was up drinking coffee early Sunday morning, sitting out on the front porch, watching the sky lighten. And if it didn't look like rain, Sid and I would hit the road. Soon I was riding both the Black Shadow and the Duke with confidence. We headed off on long trips down into the Carolinas, generally stopping at the same places and then racing to the next ferry landing.

I knew, of course, that neither of those machines would be making the trip with me back to Dartmouth, but I had my eyes on the Matchless. Sid couldn't ride the bike—it was too small for him now, and he had rejected her as inferior to his earlier Clubman. But I knew it was going to take convincing, so I concocted a plan: I would take the Matchless on a long ride and look after it myself. It would prove to Sid that I could ride it back to Dartmouth.

To keep him off the scent, I told Sid I was just riding the bike over to a friend's house and keeping it there for the weekend. In reality I would be riding it alone up to Charlottesville, Virginia, about two hundred miles away.

I set off on a beautiful late-summer day and soon was motoring through Colonial Williamsburg. To further hide my plan from Sid, I had disconnected the speedometer so he wouldn't be able to tell how far I'd ridden. That meant I had to rely on my ear to get some indication of road speed, but I knew my baby. Cruising along at 50 mph felt just right. Life was great. At last I was the "wild one," red jacket and all, with a duffel lashed to the back fender.

But then disaster struck: somehow I ended up getting fed onto Interstate 64 as I came into Richmond. Suddenly sandwiched by cars, I had no choice but to speed up to keep among the pack.

In those moments of unavoidable high-speed cruising, I quickly lost any sense of how fast I was going. I was unable to think of anything at all, in fact, as eighteen-wheelers blew by me, sometimes on either side. I was terrified. I felt the vibrations of the motor, stronger than I ever had before. I was going fast but not that fast—maybe seventy. By then I had ridden Sid's Black Shadow plenty, and on a Vincent such a speed would have been nothing. But right then I learned seventy was a different story on my Matchless: the vibrations were so intense that I found myself praying that the bike would not fly apart. I finally understood why the Vincent stood out to Sid. It truly was in a class of its own.

After that stint on the interstate, I pulled over to rest and inspect my bike, and sure enough the motor's high revving had resulted in the battery overcharging. Acid had bubbled over and spilled onto the exhaust pipe, leaving a spray of brown spots on the chrome. The oil tank, located under the seat, had also burbled over. When I wiped off the oil, the water slide decal that in pretty script read "Made in England" ended up as gold bits on my rag. Looking at those horrid brown spots on the chrome pipe made me sick to my stomach. The sight brought home just how much punishment I had inflicted on my poor baby. And I knew I was in deep trouble: there was no way Sid would miss all this damage.

Late that same day, I finally made it up to the mountains around Charlottesville. Though the sky was darkening, I decided to ride on Skyline Drive. I felt that the only way to wash away the day's bad experiences was to ride that legendary road along the top of the Shenandoah Valley before heading into town to stop for the night. I exited the interstate and merged onto the parkway.

It didn't take me long to realize that the bike's carburetion was so poor that I could barely get up and down the steep inclines; the rapid atmospheric changes were killing the engine. Performance only worsened as the chill of night began to settle into the valleys. I decided to pull off and make a carburetor adjustment. While trying to stop, I lost my footing on the loose gravel at the roadside and laid the bike over. I was mortified. But dropping a bike when coming to a stop is something everyone does sometimes. Generally, all you hurt is your ego. Most times your bike is not so lucky. As I righted the bike, I realized how tired I was: my muscles ached, my head pounded, and for a moment even looking through my bug-splattered face shield felt like too great a task. Fortunately, all I'd done was add some minor scuffing to the headlamp shell.

I went out a quarter turn on the air screw in the hopes that it would improve the erratic carburetion. While coasting down the ridge line, I had heard the motor cut in and out. Listening to those sounds, I knew that my bike's mixture was too rich. At low speeds there was simply not enough oxygen in the fuel to enable the spark plug to fire and induce combustion. I was rectifying that problem by increasing the amount of air in the mixture.

Just then a state trooper spotted me and pulled over. With my heart beating through my maroon jacket, I assured him I was fine and that I was just taking a break and fixing my bike.

He nodded and asked me to start the Matchless and I kicked it to life. Over the idling engine, he asked me to turn on the headlight. Virginia was a lights-on state.

I looked at the switch and it was in the on position. But nothing. Now my heart was pounding. I was about to get a ticket and the bike wasn't legal to drive.

I assured the officer it had been on before I stopped, and I then begged him to give me a moment to peek inside the headlamp shell to inspect the wiring.

I set to work, removing the headlamp from its shell, and spotted—to my great relief—a dislodged wire and reattached it. Satisfied, the trooper rode off.

I should have felt proud that I'd gotten away with no ticket, but instead I was totally deflated. I had constructed the whole trip as an elaborate test of my abilities and I had failed. Sure, I had corrected the mixture and found the electrical fault, but these were minor things compared to what Sid did in the shop every day. What would happen if I had to actually go into the motor? Who was I kidding? I was still a kid. The Matchless was too good for me. I was just a hack, the sort of guy my father made fun of.

When I brought the Matchless back to Sid two days later, there was no hiding the hell I had put the bike through. I didn't even bother to clean it up or to reattach the speedo cable. I simply rode it to Big Sid's, parked out front, and went inside, purposely avoiding him. He went outside and slowly walked around the bike. I watched his facial expressions change as he spotted things.

Eventually, Sid came back inside and quietly asked me to tell him what had happened. With my head down, I told him the truth. By the time I had finished, he thanked God for my safe return. It was the sort of comment that usually drove me crazy because such outbursts always made me feel like he knew I would encounter problems I couldn't solve on my own, but this time I understood. Riding alone for long distances is a real test of nerves. The thought of helping him fix the Matchless didn't even cross my mind. My confidence had hit a new low.

A few days before I was to return to Dartmouth, Sid told me over dinner that he had stopped off at Honda of Norfolk that afternoon. "Do you know what I was doing there?"

"No idea."

"I bought you a bike to take back to college."

I couldn't believe what I had just heard. Somehow, despite everything, my plan had worked. Evidently, I had hidden my lack of confidence because Sid expected me to whoop for joy. So I acted the part but deep down, now that my dream had come true, I was scared.

"Don't you want to go down and collect it?" Sid asked.

"Sure," I said, but I could hear the hesitancy creeping into my voice.

When I laid eyes on my first road bike, I still wasn't sure how I felt. It was another Honda—this time a CX500—and that alone was comforting. But it wasn't the Matchless, let alone the Duke or the fabulous Vincent. Nor was it some state-of-the art sport bike. The color scheme was a dull brown with black and gold stripes. Parked it looked drab and forlorn—totally without the glamour I had always lusted after. I walked slowly over and then settled into the seat. Just then everything suddenly felt right. I pushed the red button and heard it fire up instantly, ready to go. I pulled away and turned circles in the parking lot as I got used to the feel. Then when I got on the throttle, that CX leapt away like a goosed bull. I hit the brakes and she pulled up firmly. Drab she may be, but with its low center of gravity, that bike felt nimble for its bulk. Yet it remained planted, stable as a barge. All in all, the total package made for a confidence-inspiring ride.

Certain that I had taken to my bike, Sid explained why he had selected it. The CX, you see, is a true legend among bikers, having rapidly emerged as the bike of choice among European street couriers. A savvy Japanese copy of a stalwart Italian Guzzi design, the thing runs forever. I may have looked cool learning on a Matchless, and I loved to ride that Duke, but when you send your kid off to school, the bike messengers' ride is the one you want.

And all at once I knew I could load it up without worries. So what if it looked old and plain. In the next instant, I saw myself riding all over New England, maybe even with a girl on the back. Suddenly, my spirit and determination had revived.

Needless to say, my mother wasn't pleased with Sid's purchase because she was afraid I would get into an accident, but she agreed to let me take the bike to school, as long as I didn't ride there. As a compromise, my father paid his mechanic, Luke, to taxi me up in the shop van.

After we got to the far side of the Chesapeake Bay Bridge-Tunnel, Luke pulled over and we rolled out the Honda. He didn't ask; he just did it. Then I got on my bike, fired it up, and led. As it turned out, we ended up needing the space in the van, when, outside Washington, D.C., we spotted a broken bike beside the road.

It was a Vincent no less. Of course the stranded riders knew my father. The entire scene could have been scripted by the Marx Brothers. Luke cracked one joke after another: We were Big Sid's emergency Vincent rescue service. We hoisted their bike into the van and ferried them home. No payment, no tips please. Just keeping the world safe for Vincents.

Another Jewish Faulkner

*   *   *

After that Luke announced that we were going to take another detour. We would stop in Troy, New York, and visit with some of his old friends. I excitedly agreed. It added miles to the trip and I liked Luke. He was cool and he promised me that we would have a good time.

Only when I saw all the Harleys out front did I realize that Luke was taking me to a clubhouse. I didn't know that he had been in a gang. The situation made me a little uneasy. I parked my bike toward the edge of the lawn and walked over to the Big Sid's van.

When I got to the driver's door, I saw Luke remove a holstered handgun from the glove box and smile. Its presence came as a surprise to me, but I said nothing. Sid often carried a weapon and so did many of his friends. With a flourish, Luke laid it on the seat of my Honda. He then warned me never to carry a weapon into a clubhouse. I asked him why he hadn't just kept the gun in the van.

"Because I promised Big Sid I would look after you." Then he added, "That's a rice burner! The best way to keep it safe is to put some heat on it."

When I asked if he wasn't afraid someone might walk off with his gun, he just laughed.

Later that night when the party really got going, Luke's buddies began to poke fun at me. It started with their insisting that inheriting a Vincent "didn't count." A few more beers and it was, "You'll never be nothing but your old man's kid."

I had heard this type of thing before from bikers, and I never pushed back. In the world of motorcycles, I knew I was nothing. And once guys saw that I agreed with them, they usually stopped giving me the business. That night in Troy, they fell instead into speculating on the future of their independent club while we played poker on a small table that shared the kitchen with a Harley.

The Hells Angels had just come to town and the news had these guys running scared. The last thing anyone in that room wanted was to piss off the Angels. And you did that by making yourself a nuisance and giving bikers a bad name. That night everyone in that house wanted to keep a low profile.

Afraid, they were irritable and the mood threatened to turn sinister. Determined to lift their spirits, I adopted the role of scribe that Hunter S. Thompson had made famous and begged them to tell me all about their lives. That got them excited and soon they were talking over one another, telling me about work down at the ball-bearing plant. Then they fell into playacting their jobs for me. One guy sat and banged an invisible button; another loaded boxes onto a pallet; a third moved the pallet stacks to be packed in trucks. For them it was that or their faces in the wind.

As I fell asleep that night, I was haunted by a premonition that I was going to end up like those guys—stuck in a dead-end job and too stoned to know which way to turn a wrench. I decided then and there that I had to elude that fate. I loved motorcycles, but I was going to do something totally different from what my father did.

Back at college, and with the spirit of the newly baptized, I started writing stories featuring a poor scholarship kid coming of age and trying to fit in at a posh Southern prep school. I told myself I would escape my feared fate by becoming, instead, a famous writer—a young Jewish Faulkner. I suppose I knew even then that this material was tired, yet I was desperately resisting my father's world and ready to focus on anything else.

But all that changed when I read Thom Gunn. A contemporary of Sylvia Plath and Ted Hughes, he was coming to give a reading at Dartmouth. As I prepped for his visit, I discovered his poem "On the Move." To my astonishment, it was a meditation on riding a motorcycle and it had made him famous.

At the start, Gunn told the audience that he was in his final push to complete his latest manuscript, *The Man with Night Sweats*, and would only read from that. Then he stunned the crowd with a string of incredible elegies for the life he had lived before AIDS ravaged San Francisco.

It was a great reading. I was disappointed that I didn't get to hear "On the Move"; nevertheless Gunn's outfit had me convinced I could still get him to talk about motorcycles. The English poet looked like an extra in the Who's *Quadrophenia*. He had on a classic American-style biker jacket, jeans, and motorcycle boots. The only thing missing was a proper fifties-style riding hat.

I tailed him to the reception, where he was huddled with the poet Tom Sleigh and the novelist Ernest Hebert, both professors at Dartmouth. I waited until I saw an opening in their circle and took it. I told Gunn that "On the Move" meant everything to me.

But to my surprise, Gunn shrugged off both the poem and motorcycles.

"Really, I was just along for the ride, mostly on the back," he said. "It was the boys, you know."

I was shocked but pressed on. "What kind of bike was it?"

"Oh God, I don't know, there were so many. Besides I'm too old now." He had a bemused, slightly sad expression on his face.

"But Thom, you look like you could go for a ride right now," Sleigh pointed out.

"I always found the look attractive," Gunn admitted with a sly smile.

"Go ahead, Matt, take him for a ride."

Gunn looked at me again. For the first time he focused on my maroon suede leather jacket.

"My Honda's parked outside. And New Hampshire is not a helmet state," I offered.

"I'd throw your balance off," Gunn said. He took a sip and surveyed the room, studying the young students. "Haven't been on one in ages," he said wistfully.

I decided to break Gunn's melancholy by entertaining him with a recount of a recent ride. I had let my friends talk me into taking the Honda on a trail, against my better judgment. "Sure enough," I told Gunn, "I hit a patch of bunny hops and I bounced around until the handlebars went into a lock-to-lock and that was it. Down she went for a nap in the field."

"Lock-to-lock, eh?" Gunn eyed me seriously. "We used to call that a tankslapper."

I nodded.

"But you weren't going all that fast."

"No," I admitted.

Looking into his eyes, I felt as if I was peering into a mirror. In that instant, I suddenly realized more fully than I had ever before just how close to death I had come that day on the Duke. Gunn too was caught up in some past moment of sheer terror and dumb luck. I knew then that Gunn's first comment to me had been a lie—he *had* ridden a great deal in his life and knew just as I did what it was like to have a close call.

I pulled a copy of his *Selected Poems* from out of my jacket and asked Gunn to sign it.

As he handed back my book, he patted me on the shoulder. "Your bike *went for a nap in the field*. Hadn't heard that one in ages."

Left alone, I nursed my drink. Throughout my college career, I worked late at the medical library and often rode home after closing up the building at midnight. I felt as comfortable on those rides as I did on the Dartmouth skyway, slaloming down the middle, cutting between the dotted lines while my headlight bore a hole into the oncoming darkness. I had wanted to write a poem or two about that, and after meeting Gunn, I did.

I returned home after graduation, determined to write a novel set in the world of motorcycles. At the same time, I told myself my book could be about anything but my father. I already knew I couldn't handle a wrench, and I was really afraid that I was about to learn that I couldn't write either. The prospect of including my father in that discovery was simply unbearable.

So I didn't tell him what I was working on and conducted my research only when I knew he wasn't going to be at Big Sid's. To do that, I made sure that my visits coincided with his departure and the arrival of Stan, his best mechanic. During the day, Stan worked on military aircraft for the navy, so he would arrive just as my father was closing up. Once Sid was gone, I would pull up and knock on the glass. Stan would let me in, and I would spend a few hours helping him.

That summer Stan worked patiently with me until my skills as a mechanic greatly improved. The more time I spent with him the closer we became. He told me what a good man my dad was. I listened to his stories about Sid's gift: how he could practically speak to the machines he worked on. He stressed that Sid gets so obsessed with the Vincents, he doesn't realize just how many bikers riding everything from a Harley to a Jap bike know and respect his work.

He told me that even Steve McQueen had stopped in. Sid was out, but Stan was there. At the time Sid was trying to make a go of it as a Guzzi dealer and had a pearl white 850 Le Mans on the floor. Stan encouraged McQueen to take it for a spin, but the actor declined, confiding that his meds had ruined his sense of balance. This was right before McQueen lost his battle with cancer.

Stan could see the distance between Sid and me. But he knew that life is precious, and he wanted me to give my father a second chance. To make that clear, he told me what had happened the previous spring.

Sid had been down at Daytona, giving a talk about the art of tuning and Vincents, and had left Stan in charge of the shop. That invitation to speak remains one of the high points of my father's life. Even now Sid can describe what it was like to look out at that crowd and spot the top racers from his youth, from Dick Mann and Klamforth to "Springer"—practically the whole wrecking crew, along with many of the top mechanics.

But when Sid called to check in, Stan didn't tell him the truth. He didn't want to spoil Sid's fun, so he waited until the trip was over.

But in the course of those summer nights, while Stan taught me how to do a top-end job on an old BMW boxer, he told me. Nothing could stop him from circling back to what had happened. His son, Shane, had been born with spina bifida, and when my dad was off on that trip, Shane died—at the age of nine. Stan and his wife, Sally, were in the living room, getting ready to take him to the doctor, when he stopped breathing. Stan kneeled next to his son, who lay on a blanket on the floor. He administered CPR and then whispered to him one last time. In those moments, hugging his child, Stan said he was bathed in a warm white light and that he felt the presence of God in the room, taking his boy away.

But the lesson Stan was trying to teach me didn't take. I believed that I was on my way to a successful life as a writer, and reconciling with Sid just wasn't important to me. I had been accepted into the creative writing program at NYU. I would soon be off to experience life in Manhattan.

Before coming home that summer, I sold my Honda to a fraternity brother for four hundred dollars. It had given me three years of trouble-free service, but I let it go without a second thought. I didn't need—and couldn't afford—a bike in New York City. More importantly, I told myself, I had already collected the experience I needed to write that first book. I had ridden enough and, thanks to Stan, now knew enough about wrenching to write in authoritative detail. Hemingway's *The Sun Also Rises* came out when he was twenty-six. I challenged myself to equal that, and I had four years in which to do it. I decided I could fictionalize my two-wheeled experience faster if I made a complete break from it. So I told myself that part of my life was over.

A few months later, I traveled back to Dartmouth for Winter Carnival. When I stopped in at my old frat for a party, I spotted my Honda parked behind the house and covered in snow.

Though I tried to look away, I couldn't. The cover I had given the new owner was nowhere to be seen. As I stood still in the night air, I felt a chill work its way deep into my body. I heard my old friends calling to me to catch up, but I lingered and their voices faded, suddenly replaced by the soulless hum of the streetlamp under which my old Honda sat parked. I walked over and looked down at the instrument cluster: its dials were obscured by ice webbing under the bezels. The handgrips were caked in mud, and a thick coat of orange rust had bloomed on both wheel hubs. I wanted to reach out a hand and stroke the seat to knock off the snow that covered it, but instead I thrust my hands deeper into my coat pockets and walked away.

Chapter Seven

Getting Back On

A fter that last encounter with my poor Honda CX, I went for just about a decade without a bike. And truth be told, I never felt the pull of a motorcycle, not while living in Brooklyn. Then again, I had other things on my mind.

Martha was beautiful, funny, and, perhaps best of all, she wrote sublime poetry. We met at NYU. We both wanted to be writers, and our love took away all thoughts of motorcycles. Nor did things change when Martha won a prestigious Stegner Fellowship at Stanford and we moved out to San Francisco.

Of course I couldn't walk a block in that city without seeing a motorcycle—they're all over the Bay Area, often unusual ones too—old BMWs and Triumphs mixed in with the modern sport bikes and Harleys. I would look them over, and every once in a while I would spot a motorcycle shop and duck in. But it went no further than that. Instead I directed everything into my dream of becoming a writer.

Two years later Martha and I moved to Iowa, where she had won yet another fellowship. The Midwest's charms are not unknown to motorcyclists, but I remained uninterested. Only one thing then mattered to me—writing, novel after novel, for six straight years.

At Dartmouth I was fortunate to have lunched with Saul Bellow. The Nobel Prize winner had warned me then of a writer's worst fate: "Stories," the old master said, "he has. But not luck." Well, in Iowa I was living those words. It was a constant struggle for me just to match what Martha was bringing in from her fellowships. To do it I repaired ATM machines, temped, waited tables, and, increasingly, taught.

Finally I threw in the towel—I was no novelist. At the same time, my acceptance to Duke's elite PhD program made me realize that a future was taking shape for me—only I didn't want that life. Martha insisted that I would find the time to keep working on my novels while taking classes, and I told her she was right, but deep down I knew I was finished.

On a trip to Duke to go apartment hunting, we found ourselves entering the Appalachian foothills. Suddenly, I was surrounded by the roads from my trip on the Matchless. I looked at the lovely green woods stretching away on both sides, and desires I had pushed away for so many years washed over me. I realized what a fool I had been to deny myself the pleasure of riding for close to ten years. As we drove along Skyline Drive, I playfully demanded that Martha write a poem about the sublime landscape. But all the time, I was trying to remember just where I had fallen and where the trooper had pulled over.

After we returned to Iowa, I picked up the phone and called Sid. Then I began speaking to him maybe once or twice a month. Those conversations rarely went deeper than formulaic pleasantries. But once I admitted to him that I wanted help finding a bike, the conversation changed. The problem we came up against was that neither of us had any money to put up for it. But I had a plan. He and I would team up to write an article for a bike magazine and use the proceeds to get me riding again. Sid was skeptical that I could pull it off, but then I landed the piece for a five-hundred-dollar payday. Armed with the promise of this cash, Sid looked around. Soon he called back to tell me he had found me a lovely little V-twin, a 1989 Honda Hawk GT from—once again—Honda of Norfolk. He asked me if I wanted to see it first, but I said no, I trusted his judgment, and he went down and bought me my third motorcycle.

That bike saved my life. If I hadn't had the ability to ride every day when I made the decision to go to Duke and abandon my career as a writer, I would have sunk completely into an abyss.

Once the Hawk had reconnected us, and reinvigorated me, Sid and I talked often on the phone, and it was a rare conversation that did not end with Sid repeating his pledge to find me a Vincent of my very own one day.

I always laughed off those vows. Then Sid called with astonishing news. As incredible as it sounds, an old, intact Black Shadow had just fallen into his lap. It was a flat-out gift, given to him by a man named Lex, an old riding pal who had moved away from Tidewater decades before.

Lex had a daughter and a son, but neither had an interest in motorcycles. Sid often called Lex to talk bikes and the old days. Indeed it was Sid who had found Lex this very Black Shadow. Sid had first spotted the bike in front of Meridian Sales. It was then the property of Bugs, when he was a sailor new to town. Sid and Bugs became fast friends, but Bugs sold the bike shortly before he shipped out on long deployment and that's when Sid had spotted it for sale, for $350, in a sports car shop.

During these conversations with Lex, Sid often liked to talk about me: how much I loved riding my Hawk and how I had just gotten a tenure-track job in Louisville. Sid told Lex that he wanted to present me with a Black Shadow to commemorate this achievement. "So if you ever decide to sell that Shadow of yours," Sid told his old friend, "let me know because I would like to make you an offer."

Lex responded, "Hell, I'd rather give it to you."

By the time Lex gave Sid my Shadow, my dad had closed his commercial shop. Instead he had built a free-standing garage in the middle of our old backyard, right where I used to zip around on my little Honda. Now between their social security checks, my mother's pension, and Sid's restoration work, my parents had enough money to allow them to do what they wanted.

For Sid that meant working on a full rebuild of Lex's bike. He kept me abreast of the project over the several years it took to finish. When my Shadow was finally ready to ride, I planned to fly down to Norfolk because I wanted to be the one to break her in.

But Martha and I were trying again to start a family. Our first attempt had ended in a miscarriage, and that experience had filled us with intense anxiety. I knew there was no way I could spend the summer away from Martha just to learn how to maintain a motorcycle.

Instead I convinced Sid to drive back to Louisville with my Shadow in tow; we could do the break-in here. Our house, however, couldn't accommodate Sid. It was too small and too difficult for my father to navigate. His knees were giving out and even the front steps were spaced too far apart for him to climb them with confidence. Inside, the bathroom was too small, the toilet too low to the ground, and on and on. But after I explained the situation and did my research, Sid decided that he was willing to spring for a handicap room at a nearby residence hotel. In addition to working on my bike, he had finished up several long-term jobs. As a result he was suddenly flush with cash and unusually eager to spend it. I looked around, and found that for a few bucks we could have a nice month together.

I didn't doubt him when Sid said that he felt sick and that his life was coming to an end. It was one of those times when it was hard for me to think straight. I just braced for what was to come and told myself I was prepared mentally. Of course I felt regret and wished things had turned out differently. One thing in particular kept haunting me—that Sid would never get to see his grandchild.

Once Sid arrived, he told me he had decided that he was never going back home. When I asked why, he answered simply that he didn't want to be with my mother when he died. I thought, then, that I understood my father's motivation. More important, I saw no reason not to help him. Although my mother sometimes insisted otherwise, she knew a permanent separation would do her good, too.

Martha agreed, and in fact she was the one who found Sid his apartment. On the way to her favorite coffee shop, she saw the realtor putting a sign in the lawn in front of a complex not far from our house. It was perfect: a ground-floor, one-bedroom unit for only $390 a month.

We hadn't figured out yet how exactly Sid would support himself after he ran through his thick wad of cash, but he didn't seem concerned with such details. Nor was I. He looked sick and beaten. Long-term financial questions just didn't cross our minds. He moved into that little apartment at the start of August and on the night of September 24, 2000, had his heart attack there.

Part Three

The Build

A motorcycle is not an appliance.
No one hugs their refrigerator.

—Big Sid

Chapter Eight

Sid's Return

I'd been talking to a dead man—only he didn't die. We spent our nights in his hospital room, and as we talked I kept thinking about my pledge. Somehow he had survived that heart attack, and then bypass surgery, but what had I done about my promise to build a Vincati? Nothing.

Driving home from the hospital that night, I stopped by Sid's apartment to strip his bed and take out the trash. His car sat parked in front of the complex, under a blossom tree. Fall had come early and the windshield was covered in heaps of yellowed leaves.

While I straightened up the place, I hunted around and found his address book—a rubber-banded collection of note cards and paper scraps. I sat at his little table and started turning over the cards, looking at names in the hope of spotting one who might help me. Step one in building a Vincati would be finding a Ducati 750 GT chassis. While I dug into the pile, I thought again about a visit I had made years before. I was sitting with Sid at the dining room table back in Norfolk, with my key ring next to my plate, about to cut into a bagel. Sid spotted it and launched into a lecture about the evils of loading up your car's key ring. All that extra weight bouncing up and down as it hangs off your ignition key couldn't be good, he reasoned. He had been on me to remove some of mine but I had resisted. That morning he kept pressing me but I refused to satisfy him. I just sat there reading the paper. Then I picked up my knife and in attempting to split my bagel in half I sliced into my knuckle. Sid then began to lecture me about how to properly use a knife and how to hold a bagel. At that I snapped.

"I know how to eat. I use a knife and fork every day, thank you."

Sid clammed up.

We ate in silence and I stewed. I was twenty-five but here he was—still treating me like I was a kid. Then I left in a taxi, angry as hell, and I didn't come back for years. The next time we were together, I was up from Duke to collect my Hawk.

I had been such a hothead then.

I kept flipping address cards. Then I spotted the name of an old friend who might be able to help, a certified Italian bike nut everybody called Monsieur G.

After a couple of rings, G answered.

I explained why I was calling. Could he help me buy an early Ducati 750 GT chassis?

"If Sid wasn't in the hospital," G responded, "I'd tell you to go to hell." Then he explained my mistake. "If I start asking around for a frame and tell the guys why—that you want to chop it and put a Vincent motor in it—I'll never be able to show my face again."

As a Vincent guy, I had never really thought about how my quest would be seen by the Bologna faithful. To a Ducatista, what I wanted to do amounted to no less than the rape and murder of a beautiful frame. Fortunately, since he was the first guy I called, no one else would know what I was putting him up to. I promised him this would be my last inquiry.

"Okay," he said. "I'll you do you this favor, but on one condition. You can never say who gave you the frame."

"You have my word," I said.

"What the hell do you know, anyway, about building a Vincati?"

"Nothing," I admitted.

"Has Sid ever built one?"

"No."

"Jesus. Lots of guys have tried. Then they fuck up the frame and that's it. What about the mating plates? Where are you getting those?"

"Sid's got a line on them." Of course I had no idea what he was talking about, but I filed away the detail. I added, "G, a man has got to have something to focus on if he is going to get up and live."

"Yeah," he conceded. And then he added, "You are lucky your dad is who he is. I wouldn't do this just for you."

And with that, he hung up—though I kept on talking until I heard the dial tone.

During my next visit, Sid was able to walk up and down the hallway without assistance, and he appeared to be healing well. There was even more good news—G called to tell me he had what I needed.

A guy was building up an old 1973 GT for vintage racing, and midway through the rebuild he decided to put his motor in a Verlicchi, a well-known Italian aftermarket frame. Compared to the stock frame, the Verlicchi was lighter, stronger, and offered more agile handling. Now he was eager to part with the rest of his project, a complete rolling chassis: not just the frame but the swingarm and front forks, as well as the seat and tank, along with beautiful new eighteen-inch wheels sporting freshly laced rims and shod with new Avon Venoms. In short he was willing to sell us everything but the motor. All I had to do was hand G a check for $2,500 and pay for the delivery, and we'd be on our way.

"Dude," G insisted, "grab it. That sort of thing don't come up every day."

I couldn't afford it, but what the hell. The man was back from the dead. So I pulled the trigger.

Once I'd bought the GT chassis, I had to come up with a place to store it, so I called in another favor and had the bike shipped to a local shop called Hot Bikes. I dropped my dad's name the first time I stopped in. The owner had heard of Big Sid and was happy to do what he could for his son.

I didn't tell Sid about my find right away, knowing that deals can fall apart and apprehensive that the bike might get damaged in transport. But when the chassis arrived at Hot Bikes, it was perfect—clean, spotless, and totally free from damage.

I squatted down for my first good look at the frame.

With the image from Sid's photograph in my head, I thought about what we would have to do to make this frame accept a Vincent twin motor. It was obvious that a pair of struts (or "down tubes") were going to have to be removed. On a Ducati, these tubes extend down from beneath the gas tank and bolt to either side of the motor's base.

In contrast, a Vincent motor gets bolted to the frame not down low but up high; that is, at the top of each cylinder head. To build a Vincati, we would have to remove those down tubes and modify the Ducati frame to accept the Vincent's mounting system.

For the first time, this act of violence sunk in. To build this motorcycle, I would have to hack off those frame arms. This alteration was clearly the objectionable chop to which G had referred. Her arms!

Though I saw the challenges ahead, I left the shop feeling pretty good about the project.

I decided to break the news to Sid when he most needed it.

Ten days after the surgery, Sid was transferred to one of the hospital's rehab wings. A week later, I watched while he was subjected to another battery of evaluations. While looking over the results, the therapist told us that though he was no doctor he thought that discharge orders would be coming in the next day or so.

I looked over at Sid and saw that he was more scared than relieved. He didn't think he was ready to go home, not to an empty apartment. I told him not to worry. I had talked to his social worker and knew he would be getting extensive follow-up care. Initially, a nurse would stop by to examine him, and after that, I would be shuttling him to more rehab. But hearing me tick off these facts didn't seem to lessen Sid's fear. So I went out and bought a futon and set it up in his apartment so that I could stay over. Hearing that, Sid relaxed, but I could tell he still had no desire to rejoin the world. It was then that I decided to break the news.

In a poor display of feigned nonchalance, I casually mentioned that I had just bought us a chassis perfect for our Vincati project.

Sid looked at me in shock.

"When you stopped talking about it, I figured you dropped the idea."

"Oh, no."

Then I told him the whole story. Of course he wanted to see pictures. But I refused, telling him he was going to have to walk into Hot Bikes and look at it in the flesh.

Sure enough, Hot Bikes was our first stop after he was discharged, even before his apartment. Sid was impressed, but being Sid he of course had quibbles. For a start he hated the color—he'd never liked metallic green. He didn't like the handlebars either. Sid is a flat-bar guy. He could deal with handlebars that were drawn back and up with the slightest of rises but the ones in front of him that day went way beyond that. They were almost at the height of an old beach cruiser bicycle. He also said that the fenders were absolute crap, and he didn't like the shocks. At least the chain guard passed muster, and the seat and tank were in great shape. The wheels were perfect and the rear brake was even operational, though there was no front. The bike had come with some boxes, too, which I took away so we would have something to look through when we went back to his apartment. He still didn't have enough strength to throw a leg over a bike, let alone ride, but at least now he was talking about when that day would come.

Sid was back from the dead, though it would take me some time to realize the many ways in which he had changed. I discovered one dramatic difference while we were eating lunch at a local diner called the Twig & Leaf a few days after he came home. He told me then about his visions, as he called them.

He was seeing them around his apartment. Ghosts, he said. He told me about the hands that grabbed his feet and yanked them while he lay in bed and about the confederate soldier who swung a cast-iron cannonball into his side. Later a young girl skipped past him while he was reading in his easy chair. Finally, a Depression-era mother in a housecoat peered in at him from the hallway. Sometimes these visitants were in color, sometimes black and white.

Before the surgery, Sid had always been a thorough skeptic who loved to mock the superstitious and gullible. Now he believed, and what really scared me was that on some level I believed him, too. It wasn't that I found his old apartment spooky. The real reason was simply that my father's survival had taken my sense of reality and given it a good shake. With his return, I felt that somehow we had all stepped over some cosmic divide.

Not that I wanted to tell anyone this, most especially my wife. The last thing I needed was to have Martha wondering what to make of my father's sanity. Or mine. And fatherhood was the big topic for her then. We were still trying, and once again she thought she might be pregnant.

I looked at Sid and then realized that the diner had its orange and black decorations up. We were nearing Halloween. Martha wouldn't question Sid's sanity. She'd question mine.

At the thought, I made Sid promise that nothing would ever be said to Martha about the ghosts.

* * *

With Sid solidly engaged in his recovery, I began going for long rides on Lex, as I'd come to call my Vincent. My aim was to break her in and to get to where I felt that she really was my bike. It was November by then, and the leaves were peaking in color. Off I would ride, deep into the country, lost in thought and unwinding from all the stress. I probably put two thousand miles on the clock in just those first few weeks. On the way home, I would stop off at Sid's apartment and park it in the courtyard in front of his window. After I reported my impressions, we would go out and make adjustments.

During one of these visits, Sid announced that he felt strong enough to sit on the bike. His declaration took me by surprise. I was concerned that he still lacked the strength. But before I could stop him, he slowly lifted his leg and swung it over the saddle. A big smile crossed his face as he settled on the seat.

"Get my camera," he said.

I shot a photo while he posed with one arm on the bar and the other held high in a dramatic wave. He sent copies around the world, with letters promising that soon he would be back riding.

That wasn't all. The photo shoot over, Sid went ahead and kick-started the bike. Now that I had broken in Lex, he couldn't wait to see if he had been right about the bike—that she really was the fastest standard Shadow he had experienced firsthand. But, smartly, he resisted the temptation to take off. He wanted his first ride to be on one of his own bikes. I promised him we would soon make that happen.

In the meantime he contented himself with my rider's reports. Lex really was smooth and fast, a remarkable example and distinctive because Sid didn't tart her up. He preferred a Vincent to look like a runner, what he called a rider's machine.

Lex had parked the bike sometime in the mid-sixties. When Sid got her running again, he made an effort to retain the patina. Nothing was repainted or chromed. All the hardware was reused if still functional. The only big change came with the look of the motor. Sid chose not to repaint it black, preferring instead the naked look of the Rapide where you can really appreciate the engine.

A few days after Sid sat on Lex, I encountered my first major problem: going up inclines I felt the clutch slip. The motor would suddenly speed up and rise in pitch while the bike slowed. The clutch was failing to transfer the power from the motor to the rear chain. When I described these symptoms, Sid confessed that he had thought the springs were a little weak when he had reinstalled them.

"You reinstalled springs that had been sitting thirty years?"

Sid smiled. "I wanted to reuse as much as I could. Besides, it's your bike. You might as well learn now how to do the job while I'm still around."

Our house on Speed Avenue was nine hundred square feet with four rooms and a sloped driveway that ran into a small garage just big enough for a Model T. There were no lights in that dank space, not even wiring. At that time, the only real place I had to work on the Vincent or my Hawk was to roll it up the hill to the crest of the driveway. With the Hawk, it never really mattered. I had been riding the Honda continuously since Duke, but, though I'd covered sixteen thousand miles, I had never done any work on her at all. Nothing but new tires and a battery. Later that same fall, Sid convinced me that it was time to change the rear chain and both sprockets and that work, too, was done out on my dilapidated parking pad.

But the Vincent was from another era. To properly maintain one, you need to know how to work on it. My first attempt at tearing down a clutch went smoothly, largely because Sid was still weak and I was patient with him as he sat on an old stool and directed me step-by-step.

We talked while I wrenched, first about working outside under a tree in the shade.

"Reminds me of Johnny Marshall, the last of the three caballeros to score," Sid said, remembering that long-ago New Year's Eve bet.

Back then Johnny drove a taxi and lived in a small one-bedroom apartment not too different from the one Sid now had. Johnny had parked his Rapide, another red one, under the building's overhang, outside his window. Many times Sid stopped by to find him working on his bike out on the street corner, like I was doing.

"Did Johnny ride with Bugs?" I asked.

"Sure, we rode together plenty."

"What kind of man was Johnny?"

"Nice guy," Sid said. "You hear guys say you can sleep under a bridge but if you ride a Vincent you can still feel like a king. That was Johnny."

With the repair done, I rolled my bike away. Watching me work, Sid couldn't resist commenting about how much he absolutely loathed the idea of keeping bikes under the house in a cellar garage. It was a legacy of what had happened to his red Rapide at GG's. If I was only going to have the Honda that was one thing, but if I was going to be a Vincent man, I had to do better.

And as for building the Vincati, Sid simply laughed it off. If I wanted him to take the idea seriously, I had to upgrade. Fortunately, I could store the Duke chassis at Hot Bikes indefinitely, but if we were going to get started, we needed a plan.

Much more pressing were the arriving medical bills. I could see from the first few co-pays that we were at the start of a tidal wave. I didn't know where we were going to find the money for that, let alone build a custom motorcycle.

I felt terrible for Martha. Our lives already bore little relation to the fantasy future I had painted for her when we had fallen in love back in Greenwich Village. Being the wife of a professor wasn't in the cards then. Nor was getting kicked to the side by 'an indifferent university. Martha needed to get her first book of poems published but was having no luck. Without that she could only teach part time. Worst of all, we were now taking care of my father just as we were about to become parents.

I knew that things were only going to get more challenging. I worked and reworked scenarios in my head, searching for a way to make everybody happy. Only one option made financial sense: a house with enough space for Sid to have an in-law suite, plus a detached garage. If Sid could work on bikes, he and I could try to bring in enough money. Then Martha would not have to work full time with a newborn, and she could keep pursuing her own dream of succeeding as a poet.

I had no idea if my father was up to doing the work, or if there would be enough out there for us to do. Vincents were coveted and he was a guru, but the market was increasingly comprised of guys interested in parking motorcycles in their collection. That meant less and less real work to go around. And I still had my job at the university. I needed to secure tenure and I hadn't gotten very far.

I will always treasure talking in bed with Martha. The poet Elizabeth Bishop spoke of days when even a lowly toothbrush could make it into a poem. Nights with Martha were like that—except the subject was most often shampoo. I didn't care then—we were young, and it was all so thrilling. Later came the nights when she played out skits in the role of the child we would one day have. She told me she knew I would be great with kids, but I had my doubts. Still, when she pressed me, I always said yes.

The miscarriage, though, had been shattering. After that our talk had ripened and the summer I brought back Lex, she became direct: "Didn't I want a baby Bibu?"

I looked deep into her eyes and said yes. We were both committed. After I returned from an especially long ride to the Land Between the Lakes, Martha greeted me with the news that she had taken the test and this time there was no doubt: she was pregnant.

I hugged her and told her my plan: the little house we had would never do and she knew it. The baby's room she had long ago rejected, after I discovered that underneath the soggy closet's paint was old wallpaper slapped up with horse glue. The smell was enough to knock you out after a hard rain. The tile was falling out of the tub. We needed a new house and she needed more than ever to work on her poetry and raise our baby. The only way to do it was to buy a bigger house without increasing our mortgage payment.

"We buy a ranch that is big enough for all of us. Sid lives on his own side, and he and I work on Vincents out in the garage."

I'd brought it up before, though always as a kind of crazy possibility, a last resort if something better didn't materialize. But things had changed so quickly. What had seemed a surreal option was now the only sane one we had if she wanted to raise the baby right and continue working on her poetry.

"I'm terrified," she admitted.

"I am too," I said. "I can pull the plug. Drive him back to Norfolk. Find him a place there."

She didn't find that option any less stressful to contemplate. As we fell asleep, she told me, "I'm ready to try the grand experiment."

"We can make it work."

I got to name the baby if it was a boy. But as for girls' names, that was her decision and she was firm about it. She loved the great comic actress Lucille Ball and her grandma Lil, a kooky Greenwich Village broad. "For Lucy," she said.

It was during this time of decision making that I came to fully appreciate how much of a godsend Sid's old buddy Lex was. Thanks to his generosity, my dad now felt comfortable selling his most prized possession—the bike once reserved for me, his '47 Series B Rapide, engine number 275.

Back in the late eighties and early nineties, Sid had spent several years working with his buddy Bill Hoddinott restoring it. They built three bikes from one joint "garden shed" purchase: that B Rapide plus a replica Black Lightning and Johnny Marshall's old Vin. They sold Johnny's Rapide to a collector and vintage racer who lived on Long Island, in order to finance rebuilding the other two.

At first Sid and Bill owned this pair of Vincents jointly, but then after a few years Bill suggested they end that arrangement and he gave Sid first choice. I had ridden the B several times, and it was a wonderful machine. Over the years, Sid had promised that one day it would come to me. But now, thanks to Lex, I had my Vincent and Sid still had his Shadow.

That left us free to sell the '47 B and use the profit for the down payment on the larger house our realtor had promptly found for us. It was a nondescript ranch on Middlebrook Road in Woodlawn Park, one of Louisville's first fifties-style suburban neighborhoods. Martha thought it was drab and that it needed more than a little work, but it fell within our price range and it met our requirements: an in-law suite and a detached two-car garage.

We would have two more mouths to feed (Sid's and the baby's), but I was growing more confident that my dad and I could raise the additional money by doing Vincent work out in the garage. Indeed Sid had already lined up our first job: a beautiful early Shadow, one of the very first Vincent had made, that an old customer of his had recently bought at auction.

Meanwhile Sid found an interested buyer for his B—Keith Campbell. Keith owned car dealerships in Atlanta and was well known in vintage-racing circles. He loved the idea of owning a Big Sid bike, but he didn't want to stop at just one. He listened to Sid sing the praises of the B and then made a counteroffer that cut much closer to the bone: he wanted to swap us a pretty Rapide he had plus cash in exchange for Sid's B and his Shadow.

We had just finished eating lunch and were still sitting at the Twig & Leaf diner when my dad told me. "I'll tell him no," Sid said.

When I didn't respond immediately, I could tell Sid was shocked. He couldn't believe I was seriously thinking about letting his old Shadow go. It was always agreed that he would pass that bike on to me.

"I love that bike," I began.

"So I'll tell him no," Sid repeated.

"But Dad, I've got my own bike now. When you were in the hospital, I would go down in my basement and I would look at my bikes, Lex and the Hawk, and that's when I knew. I want to own Lex, not your Shadow."

Sid still didn't quite understand.

"I'm a young man. I don't want to pull up on my father's motorcycle. If I have the choice between riding the Shadow or Lex, it's gonna be Lex every time."

"And my Shadow would sit." Sid looked away out the diner window.

"Yes." It was logic he could grasp because it was his own. Earlier he had sold the silver Duke for the same reason—because a bike is meant to be ridden. (I had been living in Iowa then and had shrugged off the sale.)

Sid looked at me. "Are we really going to build this Vincati?"

"Come hell or high water," I said.

"Well then, what do I need this old Shadow for?"

"That's the spirit!" I said.

"Soon I'm gonna be riding the most fabulous Vincent of all!"

And that's how we said good-bye to the Shadow I grew up on. But first we had to go back to Virginia and retrieve it.

Shortly before we closed on our new house, Sid and I rented a Ryder truck and drove the 650 miles to the coast in a day. We cleared out the garage he had built behind the house. My mother left us alone for the most part.

The deal between my mother and Sid was simple, a straight swap: Sid signed over the house to her, and in return he took his motorcycles and his tools. As we drove away, I found myself hoping that my mother would now be able to heal and that someday she would realize that I was doing this as much for her as for him.

We took back the following bikes: Big Sid's Black Shadow and the '47 B Rapide, both, of course, now sold. Plus two more: his delightful 1950 Vincent Series B Meteor, and a 2000 Suzuki SV650, my dad's last modern set of wheels, and the real reason he was able to keep his spirits up while we packed up and he prepared to leave behind so much of his life.

By now, five months after his surgery, he was ready to ride again, but he only trusted himself on his SV. He needed a modern bike that was light and forgiving. He even thought about riding it around down in Norfolk before we put it in the truck, but I managed to get him to reconsider. It wasn't smart: he was tired from traveling and this wasn't the right time, especially given that he'd just packed up his life in Norfolk and was about to drive away from his marriage for good. He switched it on and smiled when it started up. Then I rolled it up into the truck and lashed it down.

Just before we got back on the road, we drove down to Honda of Norfolk and offered the general manager there, Dave Hunter, Sid's rickety old wooden trailer. Dave, who had already taken in the old Big Sid van, loved Sid, as young mechanics often do. He told me during that visit that next to my father, he was just a parts changer. Guys like Dave idolize Sid largely because computer diagnostics and modern factory-build quality have made Sid's skills a lost art. If the factory engineers could figure out a way to eliminate mechanics in the field altogether, they would do it, and guys like Dave feel nostalgia for the days when mechanics were both greatly needed and valued.

*   *   *

Once we got back to Louisville, Sid and I unloaded the truck and managed to stuff everything into the basement. As soon as I finished, Sid called down, asking me to roll the SV back up onto the parking pad.

"I feel like going for a ride," he announced.

I looked at him.

"Just up and down the street some," he added.

"You sure?"

"Hell yeah."

Sid got on the bike confidently, turned the key, and the SV came to life. One of the first things he had done after he bought it was to toss the stock muffler and go back with a Two Brothers Racing straight through exhaust. He loved the sound—hearty and deep.

"Want your helmet?"

"Nah. Just up and down the street first."

I slapped him on the back as he engaged first and pulled off. I listened to the SV roar and then vanish from sight. A few moments later, he came flashing by, suddenly sitting taller. Sid loved making a bike leap in second or third and to do that with his weight you had to get on the throttle hard. The SV's power comes on at around 3,000 rpm but it surges again as you approach its top end. Some guys will never overcome the sense of restraint that keeps you from really taking a bike up to near its red line, which on an SV is about 10,500 rpm. Not Sid. I watched him do another pass and this time listened to the sudden rise in pitch of the SV's exhaust note as Sid entered the meat of the motor's second power band. After another pass, he pulled up.

"Get the Hawk and let's go" was all he said.

Chapter Nine

The Land of the Righteous

We had no regrets about selling the B Rapide. Sid said that anytime he approached that bike he saw a large price tag hanging in the sky above it. You can't love a bike you see that way. But with the Shadow it was obviously different. A day or two before the buyer was to arrive, I asked Sid if he wanted to take the Shadow out for one final ride.

He shook his head no. "I have already said good-bye to it."

I decided then that I would be the one to ride the Shadow last. Sid agreed to come along on the SV. But as we prepared to leave Sid felt the pull of his old bike. He insisted I step aside so he could start the Shadow. It's a complex procedure that many guys never figure out, but Sid just enjoyed it.

Here's how it goes: First you have to introduce just enough gas into the cylinders so as not to flood the engine or wet the plugs. You have to listen until you hear the engine sounds change from a dry suck of air to a wet slurp, which tells you that the gas has reached the heads. Then you have to introduce just enough choke. Used as an aid in starting and during warm up, the choke is a part within the carburetor, roughly the size of a small stick of gum. Using a cable and lever, you lower the choke into the carburetor's airstream as needed. The farther you introduce this obstruction into the airway, the greater the gas content in your fuel mixture. Once an engine gets warm, you must remember to raise the choke or you rob the engine's power and run the risk of fouling the plugs.

And then you have to learn how to properly boot the bike's crank. You must first position the flywheel. When the valves shut, you are on the compression stroke, and as you rotate the lever with your foot you will feel increasing resistance as the pistons rise and squeeze the mixture above them. Then just as suddenly the exhaust valves open and the resistance vanishes. The trick is to start your leg thrust when you are just past compression on the longer of the Vincent's two compression strokes. Also, your leg's motion should be elliptical like a golf swing—not down but around the crank—and always in a controlled manner. A crazed effort can result in the bike toppling over (trust me on this). Finally, you must act without fear. The bike can, and will, kick back—an errant firing of the cylinders sends the crank backward and, like the recoil of a rifle, into your foot. (That's why in the old days bikers preferred thick-soled boots.)

Sid cursed every time he failed to get his Vincent to light off with his first effort. And he rarely cursed. But the ritual was taking its toll. For years the doctors had been telling him that his knees were giving out and that soon he would have no choice but surgery. Already the knee of his right leg—his kicking leg—was so bad that when he stood straight it angled inward. For now cortisone shots kept him able to do what he'd just done.

Once he had it idling, he handed the bike to me. I rode around the block, warming it up while he started the SV, and then we headed out. We rode to Taylorsville Lake, a nice easy ride about thirty miles outside town. There was a Dairy Queen nearby and a parking lot with public restrooms overlooking the lake. It featured some nice trails we could roll our bikes onto while we took turns posing in front of Sid's ever-present camera. That afternoon we talked about all the times we spent with that Vincent.

As we gazed out the window of the Dairy Queen at my dad's bikes, he suddenly said, "You know it's really okay. I've done everything I could do to that Shadow. It's probably time to move on."

I wanted to make him feel better.

"I know you love that bike," I said, "and I grew up on the back of it. But you will never love it like you loved your red Rap."

He nodded. "I wish I had never let that one go." Shortly after he married my mother, Sid and Bill Hoddinott had swapped bikes. The Rattler went to Hoddinott, and in exchange Sid got the bike we had just sold.

I gazed out at the Shadow. The day before I had reattached the stock seat and taken off the one Sid had made in the late seventies to better accommodate me as a second passenger as I got older—thirteen, fourteen. With just that one change, it no longer looked like our bike. That day I learned a simple truth: despite what you tell yourself, it is very hard to say good-bye to the bike you grew up riding.

After we returned home, I removed one final item from Sid's Shadow and put it on mine—a modified oil-tank cap. Decades ago Sid took an old-fashioned Weston oil-temp gauge, the kind where the dial rests at the top of long metal thermometer, and he ran it through a Vincent oil cap. My grandmother, Yetta, used to stick it in the family turkey to determine if the meat had cooked through. Sid used it instead to monitor the Vincent's oil temperature. (They run surprisingly cool.) Now that cap sits atop Lex's oil tank, and I put Sid's old seat up on a shelf, with the thought that one day, perhaps, it would see new service.

When Keith arrived with his mechanic in tow, I kicked myself silly just trying to start our newly acquired Rapide. It quit before I could even ride it around the block. Not to fault Keith or his mechanic. He told Sid up front the bike had driven him nuts and that was why he was throwing it in. Despite all this, I was confident that Sid would be able to fix everything.

But Keith was a gentleman, and he accepted the well-deserved ribbing he got from Sid for using Harley oil in a Vincent. (No wonder the bitch wouldn't run: a straight 50 is too heavy. The oil lies like honey on the flywheels, preventing you from spinning up the revs to generate the needed hot blue spark from the plug.) Even I, the Vincent novice, immediately spotted many things wrong with that machine. However, it looked show quality, with lots of pretty hardware. I saw problems but nothing we couldn't fix, and I welcomed the challenge. It would be my crash course in Vincent work, and I would emerge ready to help Sid build the Vincati.

After we settled into our new house, Martha and I began to prepare in earnest for the arrival of the baby. Though I was also excited, I saw fatherhood as marking the end of my youth. There was so much that I had wanted to do but hadn't had the time.

The Land of the Righteous

I had just started riding my Vincent, and was approaching three thousand miles. I decided that I wanted to pass that mark before the baby was born. So not long after we went out to Taylorsville Lake, I headed out alone on my own "last ride" before fatherhood.

After riding through Westport and Goshen, I turned back toward home. On the way I decided to stop at my favorite watering hole on River Road in Louisville, a dockside restaurant and bar with a large parking lot often crowded with bikers. I was still about thirty miles shy of three thousand.

As I was heading into the restaurant, I noticed another biker, dressed up in expensive leathers with lots of Harley logos, pointing at me. He was busy proclaiming to his riding buddies that I must be a rich boy, out on a toy. I paused and looked at him and sensed that he was baiting me. If I was not careful, I was about to get suckered into a fight. I was young, I said, and, yes, green when it came to Vincents, but I was not rich. I was Big Sid's kid.

Hearing that, the biker who ribbed me lost his audience. Guys there knew my dad. He stopped talking and slunk away while I promised to pass along greetings: from Rebel Mike and the Ol' Possum and some others. Then I confirmed what I knew: who was still riding and who was dead. The tension had vanished. Relieved, I got a beer and sat by myself, smoking and staring at the water. I loved to sit and just watch guys look at Lex.

Eventually, another circle of bikers gathered around me. These were the young Turks who had hung back while the old guys held court telling their stories of visiting Sid back in the shop. Now with things smoothed over, they couldn't resist peppering me with questions. Enjoying the moment, I walked them back over to Lex. Long, complex speculation had already taken place among them in the parking lot about a Vincent's unique features. Guys love how the Vincent's design allows the rider to rearrange all controls to suit his build. On the rear brake pedal you can flip the pad around to accommodate a smaller foot. The gearshift lever has a sequence of holes that allows for adjustment of its knob, so you can place it right under the ball of your foot. Finally, both sets of controls can be repositioned so the levers face rearward for racing. You slide all the way back on the seat, put your feet on the passenger pegs, and your brake and your gearshift are right there within reach. Even to this day, no one else makes features so thoughtfully.

I showed the group how you can flip the rear wheel around, essentially without tools. One of the guys asked why you'd want to do that. I explained that you can carry an extra rear sprocket on the other side, geared for inclines. When you hit the Rockies, you pull over and flip the wheel around and go up your mountain.

I walked back to the water after my demonstration, to have one last smoke. I still had thirty miles to go. The sun was setting and a chill had crept into the air. It was time.

As I left the bar, I thought about the challenges ahead—fatherhood, having to take care of Sid, my job. I once dreamed of being a famous writer. Now I just wanted to be able to pay my bills. Instead of walking around Paris, I was circling Louisville. I slowed when I passed various nightspots, looking for bikes whose riders I knew. But in the end I didn't see any. There was no reason not to go home.

I was heading back up on River Road. The water was on my left and I could see the lights of Louisville sparkling across it. I had a car in front of me and another behind me. There was no oncoming traffic.

Suddenly, two headlight beams cut across my path a few feet

ahead. Then from out of the trees, a small white Dodge Neon pulled in front of me to make a left-hand turn. The driver hadn't seen me. I was just a shadow in the black space between two cars. In that moment, I swerved the wrong way: into the lane for oncoming traffic, which of course was where the Neon was going as well. It would have been better to swerve right and maybe clip the Neon's trunk, but some things can't be undone. And so there we met, the Dodge and I, front tire to tire, at about 25 mph. The Vincent stopped but I flew on, over the hood, before landing like a cat on the far side.

I hopped up to right my bike, pulling it off the road and putting it on the stand. I heard Sid's advice in my head, too late: "If a car enters your path, swerve so as to pass around its rear, never the front. Go toward where it will have already been." As the adrenaline rush of terror passed, I felt extreme disappointment. I was so crushed to have hurt my Vincent.

Eventually, an ambulance showed up, but I was mostly fine— evidently growing up doing motocross on my Honda XR75 had taught me how to crash, because I had escaped relatively unscathed: a cracked toe and some contusions. There would be no major hospital costs or lost work time.

After I got back from the hospital, Sid and I went out to size up the damage. Looking at the bike in the daylight was almost too much to bear, though Sid was surprisingly accepting of what had happened. He started the bike and it sounded fine, but there was plenty wrong. One end of the handlebar was bent forward; the front wheel was toast; one of the brake drums was cracked. The fender was crumpled, but still Sid was unconcerned. There was no damage to the motor, thank God. Sid was amazed and saw it as another testament to the quality of a Vincent. We would get new parts and upgrade: modern rims, rubber, and brakes. With thoughts of the coming baby on my mind, I even insisted on turn signals. I had flown over one car and that was enough. All this meant that the Vincati project was pushed further back, behind Lex and the Campbell bike. But everything had to wait while we turned our attention to our first paid job, a lovely B Shadow now sitting up on our lift. One of Sid's best clients, Morton Goldfarb, had recently purchased this very rare and well-preserved bike at auction and had shipped it to us to service.

Oh, and I even remembered to look at Lex's odometer. It read 2,997.

A few days after the accident, we spent another spell in the hospital, and at ten in the morning on August 15, 2001, our daughter Lucy was born.

She'd had an irritated airway at birth, and the doctors decided to keep her under observation. From the first day, we were assured she'd be fine. After five days, she was released.

In the car on the way to our house she seemed so calm, like she'd been through this all before. Later that night, I woke up to the sound of Lucy crying. I staggered into her room, changed her, and then lay down with my new daughter on my stomach. I watched her sleep, her eyes darting about under her eyelids. I whispered to her all the ways I would be a better father than I was a man.

In the meantime, I had work waiting for me out in the garage.

Soon Sid and I found time to tear down the front end of Lex. For the first time, I labored to understand the complex construction that goes into the Vincent front fork and fork design generally. Once again dissatisfied with any conventional approach already on the market, Philip Vincent had his head engineer, Phil Irving, draw up an in-house design. Called "girdraulics," this layout clearly derives—as so much of modern engineering does—from the Indian motorcycle. Two massive aluminum-girder legs grip the front wheel without the independent telescopic action you see in most designs in use today. Instead, in the Vincent the whole arrangement moves up and down together, and that movement is cushioned and stabilized via a central hydraulic damper (thus the name "girdraulic"). On the Vincent this system is assisted by springs on either side.

Upon closer inspection, it turned out that one of Lex's fork legs had been bent ever so slightly in the accident. It was the thing Sid feared the most, because straightening those aluminum Vincent legs is a fool's quest.

Doing his best to downplay his shock and horror, Sid launched into overdrive. After an intense two-day search, he secured a matched NOS (new old stock) set for under a thousand dollars from Tony Maughan, another Vincent guru in England. We also decided to invest in a double-disc brake kit, a modification that forced me to learn how modern hydraulic brake systems work. Finally, we selected a pair of beautifully matching spoked rims and a new pair of matching Avon tires.

About a year had passed since that night we had made the pact in Sid's hospital room. We had the frame for our Vincati now and a garage in which to work. We still didn't have a motor. But we weren't panicked. We had lots of work to do in the garage, and Sid and I were confident that with patience, effort, and some luck things would fall our way.

Perhaps we would fix up the Rapide we had taken in the deal with Keith Campbell and sell it first and then use some of the proceeds to buy an engine. Or maybe we would just snatch its motor. Sid said he wouldn't decide until we had sorted through that machine and ridden it. We had lots of parts, but not enough to assemble a complete engine.

We continued our research. By this time we had learned about the mating plates G had mentioned when he sold us the Ducati frame. Sid managed to make a new friend online, a gentleman named Don Henderson, who belonged to the clique of Aussies who had built the world's only Vincatis. He had gone all over the world on his, racking up tens of thousands of miles. Gladys, his wife, told us that it was her favorite motorcycle. I was happy to hear that because I already saw Lucy riding behind me on it.

With Don now helping us, Sid was working through the construction in his mind, even down to the smallest of details. Two other Vincati owners, Phil Pilgrim and Neal Videan, also sent us some of the key pieces we would need. Their reports convinced me that we were doing the right thing. This was no untested idea. Thirty years of standout performance stood behind the Vincati. Don told one story that I found particularly inspiring. When Phil Irving saw his first Vincati, he walked around it and said that if Vincent had continued into the seventies, this is what they would have built.

So things were coming together. Soon we would have no reason not to go ahead and take that first big step: flip the frame over and cut off the front down tubes.

The next critical step would be to join the Vincent motor to the Ducati frame using three pairs of mounting plates. The largest pair anchors the rear of the motor to the frame, just ahead of the swingarm. The remaining two pairs of plates are used to secure the Vincent's front and rear cylinders to the Ducati's upper frame.

Construction of these top mounts also requires that you add two cross tubes to the Ducati frame. When this work is done and everything is aligned properly, you run four shafts through the assembly: one through each head mount and two through the rear mounting plates.

Don gave us a set of rear mounting plates and provided drawings for the top mounts. Sid sent those drawings to another American Vincent stalwart, Andy Sekelsky, in New York, who made us four top mounting plates. Once Andy's work arrived, Sid spent many hours looking at them. I would dance with my little baby Lucy and pass his chair. There was Sid lost in thought with Andy's plates in his hands. He didn't read like I did, but he had his constant stream of parts, each to study and admire. Knowing he was content only made playing with Lucy sweeter.

Finally, there was the matter of the essential cross tubes. These short pieces are cut from the excised front down tubes and then sculpted so as to lie across the top of the frame. From these two perches, the four top plates are then suspended so that a cylinder head rests between each pair. Cutting these tubes to size and then scalloping their ends to allow them to rest properly within the frame's rails would prove to be a real challenge—just the sort of thing Sid relished.

After Lucy came home and things starting to get back to a new kind of normal, Sid and I began in earnest to modify the frame. We bought a small welding unit to ensure that the plates and the cross tubes would stay put. My good buddy James Welch—a local carpenter, painter, and poet—built us a construction table for the project and a tall workbench for Sid.

Late in September, about a month after Lucy was born, Sid and I were in the midst of the last planning session before cutting the Ducati frame. We had finally disassembled the rolling chassis, secured all the parts, and gotten down to the naked frame. I had flipped it over so the legs we were about to cut were sticking straight up in the air.

Fall was coming on and the leaves were starting to turn. We were wearing knit caps and sweaters and the air felt crisp against our faces. Once we'd positioned the air compressor to his satisfaction, Sid lamented the loss of his garage back in Norfolk. There he had air-hose connections routed above all the workstations. Then he moved on to oiling his cutting tool and inspecting his carbide discs.

"You know once we make these cuts," Sid said, "there is no turning back."

"I know," I said solemnly. "Let's not screw it up."

But Sid wasn't afraid, not at all. He would never make a mistake on the cut. He was only concerned about breaking a disc. While he worked, he regaled me with tales of accidents, of shards breaking off and lost eyes. Now he had me terrified.

I watched him measure and then scribe the lines where he wanted to cut the down tubes. We were going conservative, leaving some distance in case we wanted to try again and cut a little above. There was no reason not to leave some extra length. With the tank on, it was impossible to see the little bit of tube that we had decided to retain, and Sid liked the idea of leaving them long in case we wanted to use them as attachment points for the horn or ignition coil.

When he was finished prepping his space, he looked over at me. "We're heading for the land of the righteous."

I didn't understand.

"In the old days," he continued, "when you spotted a chopper, guys would study it to see if it you could return it to stock. If you could, it wasn't a true chopper; it wasn't righteous. We called those half-assed choppers Tidewater Choppers. I don't remember why. Stanley came up with the name, I think. But everyone knows a righteous chopper when he sees it."

"But this isn't a chopper," I said. Like most young guys, when I used the word "chopper," I had in mind outrageously long bikes built around Harley motors. So from the beginning I had never thought of what we were doing as a chopper. I said to Sid, "It's a special."

"Yeah," he said, nodding his head, "that's what guys call them now."

When Sid was young, American bikers didn't make these subtle distinctions. Today a special is a custom motorcycle and unlike a chopper in that it is performance oriented. Most often it looks like some kind of race bike. But to Sid the terms are more fluid.

For a start, he is old enough to remember when you called what we were doing "bobbing."

In the fifties, when the British bikes started to make headway in the American market, the bobbing craze took off. The British bikes were faster, in part because they were lighter, and they started to win scrambles, off-road races that were the predecessors to what became motocross. In desperation, Harley and Indian riders started to modify their bikes, chopping off excess weight to try to stay competitive. According to Sid, they called it bobbing after a term used in horse racing, where trainers clipped, or bobbed, a race horse's tail. From there, the word "bobber" became "chopper."

Eventually, by the late sixties and early seventies, guys used the term even more specifically so that only those bikes that were modified into long, seemingly stretched creations were choppers. Sid could appreciate the craftsmanship and style that went into such bikes, but he was never a true fan. He preferred a performance-oriented approach. Then choppers fell out of favor among all but the hard-core Harley crowd. By the eighties the look seemed as dated as big Afros, leisure suits, and love beads. So guys abandoned the old lingo and talked instead about building specials and customs. Now it's hip again to call what we were doing "chopping." But to Sid none of that really mattered. To Sid what really mattered was rolling up your sleeves and building the best bike you could.

Before we started to make the cuts, Martha came out to the garage and told me that Lucy was wheezing again, as she had those first few days in hospital, and we had to go to the doctor right away. Sid and I immediately stopped looking at the bike and rushed to tend to Lucy.

Every few days, Lucy had been lapsing into bouts of wheezing, but this time Lucy was really having trouble breathing. She was now nearly six weeks old. You could see her ribcage when she drew in her breath, and we knew that was a bad sign. Our worries were confirmed when the results of an endoscopy revealed that she had a cardiovascular ring—an extra segment of veins running out of the heart and encircling her windpipe. As the windpipe grew, it was being strangled by that abnormality.

Martha and I looked at each other in shock. Crying, Martha whispered to me, "Is she going to live?"

"She is going to require heart surgery, but she should be okay," the doctor told us. But first we had to endure a follow-up MRI in order to confirm the diagnosis. I will never forget the size of that machine. It felt like we were offering our baby up to a god to swallow. After the

MRI, the nurse stopped us in the hall and reported that Lucy had gone into respiratory failure—thank God they had quickly revived her, but it was clear that she needed surgery now. We signed more papers and then walked with our daughter while they wheeled her over to the intensive-care unit.

I called Sid and told him what was happening. I stressed that everything was going to be all right even though I didn't really believe that. Like all of us, he wept.

Later that night I met with the pediatric heart surgeon who was going to do the operation, Dr. Yee. He told me he found this to be an interesting case and was eager to perform the surgery. He said his team did one or two a year and already had his interns focused on what was an unusual defect.

I looked at him and calculated his age. He was younger than me, I thought. How many of these surgeries had he done, I wondered? Ten? Twenty?

"What's the survival rate?" I asked.

"Very good," he said. "Over ninety-eight percent."

I asked him a technical question about how he was planning to do the surgery and he cut me off and said, "Dad, when I am in there I will keep my eyes open." Normally, I would have been offended but this time, I wasn't. I wanted the man who was going to have to save my daughter's life to have some balls.

That night neither Martha nor I slept. The nurses said that they didn't want to have to put her on a respirator and Lucy would not accept a mask. So Martha and I took turns holding an air tube, directing the stream of air into our daughter's mouth until the nurses wheeled her away for surgery.

Time slowed. Then Dr. Yee was sitting before us with good news.

Lucy was in post-op and soon we would be able to see her. Everything had gone well.

The last time I looked in on an unconscious heart patient it was Sid. Now I was looking down at Lucy. A tube ran out of her mouth and a drainage tube out her back. They had gone in through the side, between the ribs, and that area was bandaged. But she looked calm and at peace as she slept deeply despite the periodic chiming of alarms from all the machines in her room.

Ten days in the hospital followed, but finally the day came when we could bring Lucy home. Martha and I were so thankful that we stopped trying to get her to acclimate to her crib. This child needed her mother and I wanted her there with us. I told Martha this and she scooped up Lucy and laid her in the center of the bed. Lucy kicked her feet up for the first time since she was home, lifting them all the way to her face. After that we slept soundly, loving each other more than ever.

Chapter Ten

The Last Piece

A few weeks later I was outside on our front lawn, showing Lucy that there was a world outside the hospital. I had her resting against my chest, safe and warm in her Snugli. As she gazed upward at my face, I heard the sound of our automatic garage door rising. Then I saw Sid come out from his side of the house. He stood watching the two of us; then he gestured over at the Vincati frame.

"When do you think you feel up to making a start?" he said.

I was more than ready. "Later today," I said, and so it began.

Before long Sid had a good clean cut going on the first leg. Though the work was progressing well, Sid went slowly, stopping often to inspect the blade and to keep the metal cool. I could tell his mood was good and he was confident about completing this critical first step.

That's when I finally tapped him and said, "I'll have a go."

"Sure." Seems he had expected me to make the request and quietly handed me the tool. I held it in silence and looked at him for guidance. He respectfully said nothing. I was a man now. Before, he would have stood close by, poised to reach out and clasp my hand so as to guide it correctly.

Now he stepped back and leaned against the front of his car. I gathered myself, but I was nervous. I had never used an air-powered cutting tool before. Finally, I asked for advice.

Sid said calmly, "The key is to preserve a steady straight cut, carving out a tunnel, opening up a line of sight that you then use to achieve a clean cut all the way across. If you look closely, you can see how the tunnel is going, and it is critical to watch that and avoid cocking the blade. That's how you break it." I looked hard, and then pressed the trigger, sawing away the remaining leg until Sid had me stop. Then he finished the removal by hand. By the end of the afternoon, both legs were off and we had finally entered the land of the righteous.

Sid nodded. "It's joyous work." He said that often about his craft. And for the first time, I felt I really understood what he meant.

As the days went by, I became more and more impressed by Sid's expert work with metal. Most of our sessions occurred in the afternoon. I would pull up on the Hawk, back from teaching, and Sid would stop what he was doing so that he could enjoy the music of a running engine. After I hit the kill switch, I'd hang up my motorcycle jacket, take off my tie, and get to work.

The next major task was to fabricate the additional elements needed to mate the motor to the frame. First we cut two pieces just long enough to lay across the frame's top run of parallel bars—easy enough. The next step was to dress those pieces, and that required real skill. Each had to have its end fish mouthed so as to allow it to rest between the frame's top tubes.

This critical work proceeded slowly. To do it, Sid either used his ancient stand-up drill press or he clamped the tube in a small vice.

One afternoon, in the midst of this, I tapped him. "Let me have a go?" I asked.

Sid hesitated. "Are you sure?"

"Yes."

It was all he could do to stand still and not grab the tube from out of my hands. Sid stood aside, but his body language telegraphed to me his nervousness. It was one thing for him to have to watch me finish a straight cut he had started; it was another to have to watch me try to work freehand, grinding away at the smooth regular curves he had so carefully started on either side of those two short tubes made from some really hard-ass Ducati steel.

Before long he had launched into rapid-fire, detailed instructions. "Hold the tube firmly. Don't let the stone fling the tube. Apply steady but diffuse pressure. Work the edge broadly."

I looked at him. He was fidgeting like a child who had lent out his favorite toy.

Finally, I said, "What are you afraid of?" Of course I knew—that I would grind away too much and ruin the piece. But why should that matter? "We have plenty more tube," I reminded him.

"But I already put so much work into these."

"But I want to learn."

"It should look nice."

"You only learn by doing."

"I don't want to start over."

So that was it. He had no doubt about my ineptitude. And I knew he was right. I was on the edge of explosive anger—like I was a teenager again—but somehow I held it in. "Besides," I said, "Ducati fans would probably feel better knowing that we used up some of that tube after monstrously hacking it off."

Sid laughed. And I pressed on.

I slowly ground away the metal with great care. Still, my work was rough and uneven, not up to what Sid could do. But we had a long way to go before these tubes could slip into the frame. I worked some more and then handed the pieces back to Sid so he could even everything out.

One day, not long after I returned from teaching, my dad greeted me with the simple announcement that the tubes were done. I always felt sad when I missed progress being made out in the garage, but I also knew Sid was having a great time. I walked over to the Vincati and studied the pieces as they now sat hooked across the frame's top tubes. He sat with his back to me, disassembling some dampers.

"Nice work," I said.

"Hell," he cracked, "the gaps are so small welding is almost superfluous."

With those pieces able to just slip in place, Sid turned to Andy's plates. Each had a channel cut into it to allow the plate to hook into the chassis and be braced by a preexisting cross tube. These channels had to be opened out before the plates could be rotated into their proper position and locked into the frame.

Once again work was slowed by my irrepressible need to pick at Sid over his inability to surrender critical tasks to me without my asking.

Anytime I managed to do any hands-on high-skill work, he tensed up and began to fidget. Finally, I lashed out.

"Damn it, Dad, I'm not a kid anymore."

"I know, I know," he said, trying to calm me. But we were working on Andy's plates and Sid feared having to ask him to make a duplicate set because I had gone and ruined them. That conviction prevented him from backing off as he had when we worked on the cast-off Ducati tube.

But I wanted to have a go at extending the channels. He thought he had it close and was not going to let me step in.

Watching him work, I stewed in anger. So much that I wanted to scream, but I only said, "You are living in my house. The least you could do in exchange would be to let me learn."

Sid switched off the drill press and let the metal cool and the bearings rest. As he worked the belt some, testing it for any cracks or soft spots, he said, "From my two bikes you got your down payment and the remodel. What kind of house were you going to have Lucy grow up in?"

I thought of things to say but could not bring myself to say them.

Knowing he had me, Sid said, "We are both getting something out of this and you know it."

Again I tried to say nothing. So first I held out my hand. When he didn't hand me the plate, I said cruelly, "If you weren't living here, you'd be dead already. You know it. And I know it. Now give it here."

Sid placed the plate on the drill press and dropped his head as if I had punched him in the face. He stepped back and sat on his stool. I lost myself in studying the metal I was about to grind back. Eventually, I felt calm enough to proceed. I took off some and then we refitted, and sure enough I had left plenty. Sid would have to work a few more sessions to get it to fit, but I had gotten what I wanted.

Over the next few weeks, Lucy's recovery from the operation grew complicated. Initially, her voice was smoky. I was too endeared to it to realize that it might mean something bad.

But after listening to Lucy during one afternoon visit, our pediatrician recommended that she be evaluated for disabilities. A nurse stopped by our house to test Lucy and left us fearing the worst. She told us she thought brain damage had resulted from that episode in the hospital when Lucy went into respiratory failure. The doctors and nurses had said she stopped breathing for only a few seconds. Deep down I knew, even then, there was a risk and now that fear seemed realized. Once again Martha and I were engulfed in worry.

Next we had her evaluated by a doctor who concluded that there was no brain damage. The nurse had been an alarmist and Lucy's main problem stemmed simply from her having spent too much time in bed. She lacked the muscle strength to project, thus her voice was low and weak. He attributed the skill problems the nurse noted to the same cause—poor muscle tone that was the result of inactivity.

We enrolled Lucy in physical therapy. After a few weeks of hard work, our daughter's therapist, Laurel, began to show us that from out of this wounded and frail creature would spring a beautiful and intelligent girl. Never before did I appreciate how much peace comes from hearing that you have a normal kid.

✳   ✳   ✳

The longer Sid and I worked together, the harder I found it to resist giving in to the anger welling up inside. I had fought so hard to escape Norfolk. Now I was not only living with my old man but I finally had to face up to the fact that I had to accept his instruction if we were going to make ends meet. But no matter how well I knew in the abstract that I needed to keep an even keel, eventually Sid would do or say something that would set me off.

After the blowup over the plates, I held it in until a session when we were dismantling Lex in order to identify all the crash damage. Vincents are made so that you can break the bike into three pieces: the motor and two chassis components. The rear wheel, swingarm, and seat roll away as one unit, as do the front wheel, front forks, and oil tank. Doing so leaves the engine fully exposed and accessible.

I was attempting to remove the upper frame member of that bike's chassis while Sid steadied the rear of the bike so it didn't tip over. I straddled the front wheel and reached over and grabbed the handlebars on either side of the fork blades. I gave a jerk and got separation between the oil tank and the engine. Step one was done. Step two requires you to walk the entire front half of the bicycle (in essence everything in front of the seat, minus the engine) backward. Sid warned me repeatedly that this task was tricky, and sure enough, in trying to keep all that weight clear of the motor, while stepping backward I buckled. Rather than fall, I decided to place the front half back on the engine and try again. But though it had come off straight, the oil tank's two sets of ears were now locked up at an angle against the motor's two top mounts. Lex looked like a big lazy mutt with his head cocked to one side. The forward half of the frame was tilting, the front wheel hung about an inch in the air, and regardless of how hard

I pushed or jerked I couldn't get it to settle down to the ground. Instead I could feel through the bars that the wheel wanted to go left and toward the floor. I was fighting to keep the bike upright. Only Sid prevented disaster. He was seated on a chair and holding the rear stand, which in its up position did double duty as the Vincent's rear fender brace. But even with Sid serving as an anchor, what I had done was enough to send the entire thing crashing to ground.

Now we were stuck, uncertain what to do except to hold on. In the silence he and I looked at each other.

"I can't hold it by myself," I admitted. I hoped he would have some miracle solution in mind.

Instead he snapped, "What a stupid idea this was!"

It was my idea and that was all it took. I yelled back, "Shut the fuck up and let me think."

"And do what? Figure out a way to finish her off?"

At that I went ballistic. "Finish her off? What the fuck did you ever finish? College? Sending my mother out to work? To earn the money you always promised but could never deliver?" And on and on until I got tired from screaming and stopped.

We were both still struggling to prevent the motorcycle from collapsing and fighting was only making things worse. Then it dawned on me: I told Sid to spin the bike in place ever so slightly until I could grab a tie-down strap from the lift. Then we rotated it some more until I could take the strap and loop it around the center of the handlebars and then around the bench vise as, in effect, a hook. After that I could let the bike hang. Then while Sid steadied the rear of the bike, I walked away and grabbed a tire iron. I levered apart the front end and separated it from the rest of the bike. Then I walked it over and left it to rest against the wall.

The Last Piece

To Sid's amazement, my plan had worked.

With disaster adverted, I relaxed. It hit me then how badly I had acted. Setting the bike slowly on the ground would not have been the end of the world. I vowed once again that I wouldn't lose my temper with Sid, but it wasn't a promise I'd be able to keep. The funny thing was that though neither he nor I would openly address my anger, each of us kept baiting the other into fights over nothing.

And when I started to gripe it would set him off. At this point he knew not to cross me, so instead he would try to outdo me in a pity contest. At least I had a loving family. He had married a woman who never loved him. And on and on.

Soon, when he took just two steps down this path, I would tell him to let it go.

One afternoon I snapped, "Either talk about something else or shut up."

At that he looked at me long and hard. "How can you be so cruel?"

I laughed. "If I were cruel you would be living on the street."

These fights were worse than any of the ones we had when I was kid. In the abstract I understood my goal: to be the bigger man. I had made a decision and entered into this living arrangement. I knew going in it wasn't going to be easy. But no matter how often I reminded myself to stay calm, when I was out working in the garage my anger would seep out. And it wasn't just about me, him, and the tools. That issue, I now realized, somehow tapped into how I felt about so much of what happened while I was growing up and how that still shaped me today. I never took it out on Martha; I never even raised my voice around Lucy. But in the garage I really let Sid have it.

* * *

By the time we got Lucy settled into her new muscle-building routine, the parts for Lex had arrived. Now Sid and I worked quickly to get my Vincent back on the road. We put the tire and tube on the front wheel, work that Sid could never have done on his own because he lacked the strength to force the rim within the rubber tire. I generally did this sort of backbreaking work. I sought out the pain. Of course for years there had been machines to do this work. Sid even had one in his old shop, but he preferred to do Vincent tires by hand because he thought it the safest route to protect the tube from puncture.

The next step was the reassembly of the front forks around my new wheel. Sid replaced the stock headlamp stays to bring the bucket in closer to the forks and lower to the ground, thus improving road manners. After building up the front disc system, we replaced the rear wheel and added the turn signals.

While we worked, I asked Sid more questions about the bike's history.

"How much did you and Bugs ride together?"

"At first often. All the time. He rode hard and fast."

"When did you first realize you wanted this bike?"

"When Bugs and I rode down to Daytona Beach to watch Tommy race. We did a thousand miles in one day, holding speeds well over 90 mph. We switched off several times, and though my red Rapide was faster, this Shadow was much smoother."

"How many other trips like that did you two take together?"

"That was the only long one."

I looked at Sid and sensed something. "Why?" I asked quietly.

Sid looked at the rear wheel we were fitting. "He and I became great friends. We were going to go to the Milwaukee School of Engineering. I was going to use my GI benefit. We had it all worked out."

"What happened?"

"My father," Sid said. "The bastard." He spit the words out.

"You told him on this trip."

Sid nodded. "When I backed out, Bugs did too. Instead he re-upped in the navy, and when he shipped out, he sold the bike. Years later I heard he was killed in a car wreck."

"And then Lex bought it."

"I spotted it in the window of a sports car shop downtown, and I told him to go buy it and he did. For three hundred fifty dollars."

It was Thanksgiving when we finished this job and prepped the bike for a test ride. That Sunday I rolled Lex out for the first time since the accident, started her up, and took her round the block for her maiden voyage. Martha took our baby out to the edge of the front yard to wave. At three months, Lucy had her one special toy—a large red and black lady bug. As I zoomed past she shook it and I watched its mirrored belly flash.

Even though I couldn't take Lucy with me for that ride, I will always feel that she was there to enjoy it. Done right, getting a bike back on the road after a spill is pure joy. I felt as if a great burden had been lifted: Lex was not only good as new—she was better. Any residual anxiety I had from the accident vanished, and as I headed out of the development for a genuine shakedown run, I experienced a renewed rush of passion for riding my Black Shadow.

But now Sid and I had to turn our attention to paying work. Riding season was over and money was getting tight. We had made a good start on the Vincati, enough to put her on hold, and we still had lots of things to talk over about its design and its construction. Our talks often lasted long into the night. But it was time to make some money for the family.

The first thing we did was finish sorting out the Campbell bike. We had yet to evaluate the machine Sid and I had just taken in trade. In practical terms we needed to know how much money it was worth if and when we needed to unload it. But if things went by my script, that day would not come until long after Sid was out riding his Vincati. In brief, I wanted this bike to take the place of the Black Shadow Sid had ridden for over three decades.

In looks the Campbell Rapide appeared up to the task: it was pretty, but when it got here, it barely ran. When we first began to work, I was confident that Sid could transform her in a snap. I had no fear, even when Sid finished his initial examination with the simple comment that here was a case where damn near everything was wrong. I was stupidly happy, in fact, because I wanted this bike to be my crash course in Vincents.

And that part of my wish came true. We toiled for days: magneto service and carb replacement, rebuilt gear change assembly, clutch, timing chest, rerouted all cables and hoses. When we were done, Sid kicked her to life and told me to take it for a spin and come back with a rider's report.

I headed out on my standard route along the river. Immediately, I could tell it wasn't the equal of Lex or any of my dad's Vincents. Still I wasn't alarmed. After all this was only a lowly Rapide, and Sid and I hadn't even gone into the guts of the motor. More unnerving, though, was the funny sway I felt through the seat. Then the motor made such a racket starting around 65 mph that I eased off to a tepid 50.

With a sick feeling, I headed back and found Sid sitting on his stool.

"Pretty good," I said.

He waited for something more intelligent, specifics.

"It feels normal to me until you really get on it."

"Really?" Sid showed concern.

"Yeah," I admitted. "And it shakes up there too."

"Jesus" was all he said in a low tone.

"But so what?" I added cheerfully. "We'll fix it."

Sid stood up and grabbed his helmet. "Let me ride it. Get out your Hawk."

We rode off and I led Sid to the bar on River Road that we used as a good turnaround spot. I hopped off. Sid called me over to listen to the Rapide's motor.

"Can't you hear that whine?"

I looked at Sid and then thought I heard it: a low grind beneath the normal racket. "Now you know what worn mains sound like."

"So what do we do?"

"Find another owner."

At that my heart sank. I had been confident that this bike would be a good replacement for the Shadow. I was wrong.

We walked into the bar and ordered Cokes.

"So," I began, "worn mains . . ."

Sid frowned. "Guys ride on worn mains for thousands of miles. A Brit would call these 'pitted,' actually. It's not the end of the world. It just doesn't make for a pleasant ride. And you can always change them. Just a matter of splitting the cases. It's the shudder I'm concerned about. It feels like the goddamn chain is jumping teeth."

"You don't think the frame is bent?" It was my worst fear.

And Sid's too. "Fixing a bent rear frame on a Vincent—that's like straightening a front fork. And I believe you know something about that. It can't be done."

"So it's bent?" I felt sick to my stomach.

"I didn't say that. I don't know what it is. I just said I have never felt a Vincent sway like that. It feels like a death trap. No wonder he wanted to get rid of it."

"What is it?"

"I don't know." He looked at me. "We are just going to have to take it apart and see."

"That or a new owner?" I repeated dumbly. "And at what price?"

"Hey, I was only joking," Sid said. Then, more seriously, "Don't worry. When it comes to bikes, I can make the dead walk."

We launched into a total teardown, looking for the cause of that sway Sid had never felt in a Vincent before. We started with the front forks. I took apart the spring boxes and out plopped not just greasy springs but a stack of English coins from the fifties. When you want to stiffen the springs, you add "preload," additional material or spacers, into the tube to further compress the springs when they are at rest.

From this discovery, Sid suspected we had a high-mileage sidecar bike. Now he began to think about how running a sidecar might have led to that awful shudder. We removed the rear swingarm. Sid examined the bearings. His eyes grew big. "Pure junk!" He handed me the pair. As I took them I knew I was being tested.

Finally, Sid broke the silence: "Look at the outer race."

Sid taught me then how to remove the roller races and inspect them for what he called "brinelling"—visible wear patterns, deep

Big Sid and his friends (left to right: Willie Wooten, Sid, Johnny Marshall, and Mac McCowan) at the Hague in downtown Norfolk, Virginia, around 1955. (*Sid Biberman Collection*)

Sid on his Vincent Rapide at the Richmond Virginia Fairgrounds around 1955. (*Sid Biberman Collection*)

The race between Big Sid and GG, at Suffolk Raceway, 1956. (*Sid Biberman Collection*)

Rider Paul Hall launches Big Sid's Rattler off the start line at Suffolk Raceway in Virginia, in the fall of 1960. (*Sid Biberman Collection*)

Matthew, age six, alongside an original Fritz Egli Vincent powered special. (*Sid Biberman Collection*)

Sid's rebuilt Ducati 750 GT with Matthew, age thirteen, in the background. (*Sid Biberman Collection*)

Matthew, age twenty, at Dartmouth College on his Honda CX 500. (*Courtesy of Adam Usadi*)

Matthew and Big Sid inside their garage in Louisville, Kentucky. Behind Sid is Matthew's Black Shadow ("Lex"); on the left, raised, is the Vincati. Parked on the floor is Morton Goldfarb's Egli, awaiting repairs. Matthew sits on Sid's 500cc Vincent Meteor. (*Bob Hower/ Quadrant Photography*)

Views of the Vincati, including the engine (top left), Matthew up on the Vincati at the end of an autumn day, riding along the Ohio River just east of Louisville, Kentucky (bottom left), and a look at the rider's perch (opposite page). (*Bob Hower/Quadrant Photography*)

Lucy, age seven, on "her" bike. (*Bob Hower/Quadrant Photography*)

Matthew, Sid, and Steve Hamel with his Vincent racer during the 2005 BUB meet at the Bonneville Salt Flats in Utah. (*Wendy Hamel, courtesy of BUB Enterprises*)

groves scored into the metal, in this case the worst Sid had ever seen in a Vincent.

Sid was certain. "That's the cause."

So it wasn't the frame—I was relieved. "And fixable?"

"Sure." Sid studied the machine. "What miles it must have seen, lugging that sidecar. Decades of hard use."

After a few more work sessions, I took that Rapide for another test ride. It was transformed. When I got back I told Sid, "The shudder is gone and she handles beautifully."

Sid was pleased, but the bike still didn't have the pep he loved in a Vincent. And now I too could hear the whine. It filled my mind with images of its former life, like a ghost. Vincents can rack up astounding mileage. What we had was a bike the Brits called "clapped out." It must have run perhaps three hundred thousand miles since leaving the factory. It was still fully functional—just in need of a total rebuild. We knew then that its motor simply was not suitable for the Vincati. But thanks to Sid's work, we now felt comfortable selling her for what she was: a pretty Rapide that did everything fine but had seen its better days. The way forward, we decided, was to ready the bike for a quick sale, something to hold in reserve for when we needed a cash injection. I was disappointed, but the project had become so engrossing that I surrendered much of the guilt I had felt about the sale of Sid's Shadow.

With that problem solved, we went back to our first job, the B Shadow owned by Morton Goldfarb. While Sid examined the bike and I took notes about what we would need to do, I thought about how all Vincents were hand built.

"Do you know who built Lex?" I asked Sid.

"Alan Rennie was the builder," Sid said. "Lex told me that just the other night. He had ordered the records for the bike years ago."

"You're kidding," I said. "Rennie is the guy who gave you the tour of the factory."

"Hey, you know, you're right." Sid hadn't made the connection, or had forgotten it.

Sid continued, "That's an odd coincidence. But that's how it is with Vincents."

I nodded. I had been around Sid long enough to know the truth when I heard it.

"You remember my stories better than I do."

"The good ones I remember."

"I didn't even know you were listening," he said.

Over the course of his career, Philip Vincent probably made fewer than 12,000 complete machines. About 7,000 of those are the legendary twins, with the rest being what were once regarded as lowly singles. According to club records, Vincent shipped a total of 1,072 motorcycles into the United States. Certainly, many others have found their way into the States through other channels. But still, even after factoring in those additional machines, I think it is safe to say that Sid has probably worked on most of the Vincents in America at one time or another. And as for the rest, they all have probably passed through owners who at some point picked up the phone and gave Sid a call, to source a part or get some advice about how to conduct a repair. These days, when owners bring us bikes, it is often after a purchase. They are new to Vincents and so they just bring us every scrap the previous owner gave them, and inevitably we discover traces of Sid's previous involvement. I've lost track of how many times I have held a beat-up cardboard box of used Vincent parts and spotted my father's youthful script on it.

The Goldfarb B Shadow proved to be one of the most intact Sid had ever seen. It still had the original spark-plug caps on it, the Lighthouse high-beam switch, and the Feridax medallion on the seat. Everything was correct. But it had been sitting, unridden, for a very long time. We set to work to fix that.

After making some headway on the Goldfarb B, I let Sid order after-market fiberglass fenders from Syd's Cycles for the Vincati. In another one of those funny coincidences, the oldest name on the East Coast for Ducati parts and service was a man named Syd, who operated with his son out of Florida. My dad had done business with them since the seventies. They made fantastic pieces.

A few days later we were out in the garage, evaluating the new fenders. I had been thinking about Sid's comment, "I didn't even know you were listening," and I decided to try and talk to him about it. "You know, I didn't go to Dartmouth just to get away from you and motorcycles."

"That's what it seemed like to me," Sid said. He was studying the fenders to determine where to drill the mounting holes.

"Remember that great trip we took up to Shadow Lake?"

"Sure. You had fun on that trip?"

"It was probably the best trip I ever took as a kid."

Sid stopped playing with the rear fender and acted stupefied. For the first time, I laid it all out for him.

The Shadow Lake Rally in Ontario, Canada, was the first of the big international Vincent rallies. We went to the inaugural in 1977, when I was ten. I remembered that trip not so much for passing through New England as for the fun I had at Shadow Lake.

Phil Irving was there, along with Paul Richardson, Rollie Free, and Gene Aucott. Sid remembers their conversations vividly even now. Irving talked about drawing up the engine for Jack Brabham's championship-winning Formula One racer, and how he taught Fred Astaire to drive a sports car for the film *On the Beach*. Free, too, was an endless reservoir of racing stories, and Aucott, Vincent's first American dealer, worked out of Philly and remembered Bugs and his tragic death. All this was vague to me, however—what I remembered was how much I loved the game room and swimming and the bonfires at night.

We went to Shadow Lake again in 1982. By then I was a sophomore at the Norfolk Academy, and I was dreaming of college as my out. On the way up, we stopped off at Buzzards Bay, an enclave of millionaires just outside Boston. It was a bittersweet experience for my father.

"I'll never forget that night," Sid said.

We had stopped off to deliver a Vincent to a rich collector, Ted Pratt. Much earlier Pratt had bought Sid's drag bike, the Rattler, from Bill Hoddinott after he too gave up the dream of taking her to the salt flats.

Sid said, "I remember I parked the bike in the bay Ted had left open for it. Then I wandered through this big old barn, looking at all his bikes until I found my Rattler. It made me so sick to see her. She looked even worse than when I walked her back from GG's. The seat was green with mold. I'll never forget that."

"Then, do you know what he did?" Sid said. "Pratt swapped my drag bike for a friggin' Harley Sprint."

Made in Italy by Aermacchi, the Sprint was an ugly duckling that was never taken to heart by the Harley crowd; it was the kind of thing collectors often loved best, and Pratt, who already had a handful, had to have another, because this one was in the box. So for that he let Big Sid's Rattler go. Another Vincent stalwart, Bill Easter, now has that bike, and it is as it first was, a lowly Rapide, with all its exotica removed by West Coast legend Mike Parti, who did the restoration.

"By the time we left Buzzards Bay, I knew I wanted to go to college up there. The trees and the scenery were beautiful. That's why I went to Dartmouth."

"I never knew that," Sid confessed.

"And at Dartmouth I would study in a room where on the wall there was a collection of rare gemstones donated by the Pratt family. I used to go up to the display case and examine them all the time and think about that trip."

We went back to marking the fenders where we would drill the holes to attach the stays. Outside the leaves were collecting in drifts. I hadn't found the time to rake.

Sid called me over to his side of the house a few days later. "You are going to want to sit down for this. I just spoke with Lex. I think we just found our motor for the Vincati."

"Really?"

"Lex wants to give us his Rapide."

I was shocked. Of course I knew Lex had that bike. At first he had bought it as a backup bike to his Shadow. Then in the mid-sixties, Lex had parked his Shadow and rode the Rapide instead. Initially, he had planned to overhaul the Shadow. It, too, I learned, had suffered from worn mains and the ride, Lex said, had gotten increasingly rough. As the years went by, he just never got around to servicing the bike. Instead he had given it to us.

"I sent him the tape of you riding his Shadow with the new disc brakes, and he was so thrilled he says he wants us to have this one, too."

It was another amazing gift from a man who had already given us so much.

Lex lived just outside of Chicago and we arranged to rent an enclosed trailer to retrieve the Rapide. He had an old farm with a huge barn and a small oddly shaped house that dated back to about 1900.

Lex had never farmed the land, but he did grow champion roses and a large area of the field was lined with rows of rosebushes. They had gone ungroomed for some time now and were stretching out in their wildness, their slim branches curling into unkempt wreathes that hung in midair.

The main room was an octagon and Lex sat on one side, an oxygen bottle at his feet. The floor was covered in stacks of magazines.

Lex stood up to shake our hands. I was surprised to see how tall he was. I had only seen photos of him on a bike so I had no idea that he would tower over me. Sid asked where his son was, and Lex said Jeff would be back from the city soon to help us load the bike. In the meantime, Lex wanted to take us out to dinner.

We drove to an upscale hotel restaurant, where the hostess welcomed Lex by name and showed him to his regular table overlooking a lake. While the dark water was swallowed by nightfall, Lex and Sid talked about Lex's car and the oxygen tanks he wheeled with him wherever he went. Lex never smoked and knew that he was paying the price of a lifetime of work around aircraft engines. But he had no bitterness about it. The air force had promoted him into the officer corps and he didn't even have a college degree. Before he retired, he had a hundred mechanics under him. He invented a firing mechanism for jets that was classified as top secret for years. It was based on a trick he had learned from a BSA motorcycle.

After dinner we drove back to the house to meet Jeff. I liked him immediately. Jeff told Lex and Sid to go inside and catch up some more while he and I loaded the bike. Sid agreed only after plying me with reminders about how to properly secure a Vincent.

The bike was parked in a large barn complete with a hayloft. Jeff pushed back the old sliding door and there sat a grungy but complete Vincent Rapide—the answer to our prayers.

I walked around the bike, examining it. Over dinner Lex told me why he had parked it in 1980. He had been riding it for years with no problems. But Lex had an enemy then who worked on the same base, and a buddy told him that a load of sugar had been dumped into his gas tank. Lex rode it home and was going to flush his fuel system, but the bike just sat while he rode his BSA instead. When I first laid eyes on it that night, I couldn't believe what I was about to cart home. The Rapide looked ridden and well used, but it was complete and undamaged and all in one piece.

Finally, I said, "You don't know how much I appreciate this. I promised Sid we would build this crazy bike, and without this engine, we can't."

"And then what is your old man going to do with his time, huh?" Jeff joked.

"Exactly."

"No, it's great," Jeff said. "This is what Dad wants. He doesn't have much time left; the lungs are almost entirely given out. He is tying up loose ends."

"And you are comfortable with this?"

"Sure. I don't care about bikes. And I'm going to have plenty of money from Dad. This place is three acres—we own all the woods back there. Developers have been waiting for me to put this property up for years."

"Are you going to sell all of it?"

"Nah. I'll keep this lot. Knock down the house and build my own place."

"Sounds great. You deserve it."

"Coming from you that means something. It takes a lot of work to keep these old guys going and to see them off right."

After loading the bike, we went in and joined our fathers. After Jeff said good night, I asked Lex outright if he was comfortable with what we were going to do: remove the engine and put it in the Vincati.

"Hell yes" was all he said.

Then I promised him we would use the chassis. "After the Vincati is done, I am going to buy a Vincent single engine and build that bike up to take to the track," I said. Then I asked, "How fast did you ever go on your Shadow?'

"About 125 mph. The road was as narrow as a rubber band."

*　*　*

The Last Piece

When Sid and I got in the car, he said to me, "I'm glad we did this. I'll probably never see him again."

As I drove through the night, I looked over at Sid, who had nodded off in the passenger seat, and I thought about Jeff. He was single and looking after a man who needed to have oxygen bottles dropped off every day.

Then I thought about how poor a job I had done in the same position. I had to control my anger and bitterness better. Sid didn't mean to make things worse. I needed to focus on the positive: we had the chassis and now the engine. We had come so far. I needed to start focusing on what Sid could do, instead of what he couldn't.

I told myself I would do better. I put on Dylan's *Blonde on Blonde* and settled in. I relaxed to the soothing sway behind me of a trailer loaded up with that final missing piece. While I quietly sang, I found myself dreaming of the day when I would be out riding with Sid. I would look over and there he would be: up on the Vincati, this miracle machine we had built together.

Chapter Eleven

The Mechanic and the Professor

Shortly after we returned from our trip, Sid and I decided to prep the donor bike, which had been sitting for twenty years, in order to see if she would run before we broke her down to free up the motor. Lex had told us it ran fine when he parked it, and after only a few kicks, the motor sprang to life on a magical and mild January day. It was the perfect way to ring in the New Year, 2002.

Little did I know, however, that Sid and I had dramatically different plans for this motor. I thought we would simply take this engine, largely as is, and bolt it up into the chassis. If we worked rapidly, I could imagine Sid riding around Louisville on the Vincati before the end of the coming summer.

Sid, however, had other plans. Not that he told me.

In the meantime, when I taught my students I often found that my mind remained with Sid back in the garage. As winter turned to spring, we took in an old Triumph to tune, another Shadow to revive, and a growing waiting list because he and I agreed that we didn't want to work on more than two paying jobs at a time. Then there were the little jobs: damper rebuilds, clutches, carbs to set up, parts to locate and sell. Soon I smelled of gas and sweat in the classroom, and my books had black fingerprints on the pages.

On days when we weren't out in the garage and I wasn't teaching, Sid and I would take care of Lucy while Martha went to work. I had been anxious at first that Sid would not find the prospect of taking care of a baby exciting, but very quickly he proved me wrong.

Lucy had a set of exercises to build up her strength after her surgery, and Sid and I would do them with her on a blanket in front of his easy chair. We fell into playing keep-away games where I would entice Lucy to crawl toward me to seize a little rabbit that moved back and forth on a stick like a metronome. At the last instant, I would toss the toy to Sid, who would place it down at his feet, and suddenly Lucy would reverse direction and crawl toward him.

While we played such games, Sid and I would talk, usually about what each of us could remember about growing up. According to Sid, he had been a very inquisitive child with a wide range of interests. In addition to his fascination with motorcycles, he loved to read science fiction and to conduct experiments with his chemistry set. He taught himself how to hypnotize people, too, and got quite good at it.

Most of all he loved to sing. He surprised people with the quality of his voice and its richness. Back in his prime, most of the time when we rode I listened to him sing snatches from his favorites: Sinatra and Nat King Cole.

The Mechanic and the Professor

During one play session with Lucy, Sid decided that he would sing for her. But as he launched into "Mona Lisa," Lucy frowned and then covered her ears with her hands. Sid pressed on, singing more loudly until Lucy burst out crying. I reminded him that she was still overcoming the trauma of heart surgery and that she was just learning how to integrate all sorts of experiences.

Sid stopped, and looked chagrined. But being Big Sid, he didn't give up. Often when I would leave Lucy with him for a moment, I would return to hear him singing as quietly to her as he could.

Once we finished up with Goldfarb's bike, we took in another nice Black Shadow, what British bikers call a "bitsa." Owned by Joe Walsh in Wisconsin, it had been cobbled together from various bits, a Series B front fork, Lightning rims, lots of goodies.

Of all the machines we have worked on, this was the one that most strongly seemed to regain a personality from out of the past—it was truly a rakish bike. In my mind I saw it years ago at the height of the café racer cult. Then the game among bikers in London was to pick a song on the jukebox at the Ace Cafe and race out to their bikes and roar off to Box Hill and return before the song had finished. When the police pulled up, there the bikers would be, inside, innocently having a drink and a smoke. I was certain that this Shadow had done such things.

When Joe was on his way to reclaim his ride, I took the bike out for a last little spin before proceeding with a final round of polishing. To my mounting anxiety, I started missing shifts. I headed back in first gear, determined to have Sid spot the problem.

I pulled up and waved my father over. "There is something wrong with the shift," I said, without getting off the bike or killing the motor.

"It's nothing," Sid insisted. "You know Vincents are poor shifters."

I pulled out onto the street and rode the bike back and forth in front of our house until I missed another shift and coasted to a stop right in front of Sid. I knew enough then to be certain we had a problem. I looked at Sid sternly until I saw in his face acknowledgment that I was right. I said, "You're the mechanic. What's wrong?"

Sid thought for a minute, removed the inspection cap off the engine's primary cover, and had me squeeze in the clutch. I saw him watching the interrelated subassemblies moving away into the depths of what he couldn't possibly see, tracing the flow of movement. It reminded me of this trick I used to watch him do to amuse his mechanics back in the shop days. In a campy imitation of an old midway magician, he'd lay his hands on a bike that wouldn't run and predict out loud what was wrong with it. Most of the time he was right. And sure enough, after a few minutes of looking into the primary compartment of the engine, he divined an answer.

"It's the bearing lock ring—the Loctite failed, and it's unscrewing."

The clutch is a truly ingenious device: it works to interrupt the transfer of power from the motor to the wheels. This interruption enables the shifting of gears within the transmission. In a Vincent, the clutch's shaft turns within a bearing that rests within the primary's inner wall. That bearing is secured by a lock ring. At the factory, this ring is threaded into place until tight and then secured with a cotter pin. Sid could not get the holes in the ring and the bearing carrier to realign and so had resorted to red Loctite. But the thread locker failed, allowing the ring to unscrew, causing the clutch to malfunction.

We looked at each other as we thought through the work we were going to be doing in the next hours: the entire primary had to be torn down; the clutch had to be removed until we got to the transmission door and part number G45, the bearing lock ring. Then we were going to have to do the job right and drill a new hole and fit a cotter pin.

"We are going to have to tell him to turn around," Sid said.

"Hell no!" I responded. "He's got cash in his pocket and we need it. You used to tell me you took your Vincent apart for fun and mixed the parts up and rebuilt it just to pass the time. There's no reason we can't do this."

"I was a young man then."

"Well, I am a young man now, and we are going to fix this bike."

By the time we had that bike back together, it was pitch-black. Sid had expertly drilled the smallest of holes and we had the cotter pin in place, its two ends artfully split and curled. We hadn't eaten dinner, but I insisted that before we went in for the evening, I'd ride the bike once more to check if it shifted properly. Down the street I disappeared, and the machine responded like it was roaring around the darkened lanes of merry old England with the bobbies in hot pursuit.

"Well?" Sid said, when I returned. I teased him as I sat there astride the bike, reviewing the ride. Finally, I said, "Irving would approve."

"It's shifting?"

"Slick and quick. Click, click, click."

Sid laughed and clapped me on the back.

I said, "You know, you are really are a hell of a mechanic." After a pause I continued, "Yeah, a really good wrench, but a lousy teacher." I thought I was joking, but when it came out, I realized it was true.

Sid sensed it, too. I could tell what I'd said hurt. "But all the guys ask me for advice, and I have been giving it for fifty years!" he said.

He was right of course. But that was not my point. Without getting angry I said, "I'm not talking about when you trade tips with other experienced mechanics. I'm talking about when it comes to actually teaching something to a guy like me."

That got a rise out of him and he batted back my words. "You mean a guy who can't remember which way to turn a wrench."

"Exactly," I said. I laughed because I realized I had finally arrived at a point where I could accept Sid for who he was. Thinking hard about what Jeff was going through with Lex had started to teach me how to reign in my anger, but not how to let it go. Suddenly, though, I felt released from its grip. I was never going to be able to hold a tool in my hand and be just like Sid.

But Sid wasn't done yet with me. Now he was the one who was angry. "Well, you may be a good professor but you are a lousy mechanic."

In the past I would have taken the bait. But not this time. I just smiled and said, "That's me and don't I know it." From Sid's expression, I could tell he was coming to similar realizations. And there, in our Spartan cinderblock garage, we finally understood each other.

Sid always wanted to start a work session on a customer's bike. So it was only after we had a couple of bikes in the garage to service, plus a solid waiting list, that he felt comfortable peeling off time for what he saw as our reward, our side project—the Vincati. First I gave the donor motor a good exterior cleaning. Then we moved it into position so that we could proceed with final fitment of the plates. We didn't have any pulley system or engine winch, so I slid jacks under the motor and cranked it up while stabilizing it with tie-down straps wrapped around the top rails of the frame. For better or worse, this was another strong-man job I relished doing.

Sid and I played with the motor's location until its four sets of holes aligned nicely with the mating holes in our frame. Our job was to ensure that each shaft passed through its holes without any stress. One by one we would insert the four shafts—one through the top of each cylinder head bracket and two through the rear of the engine. Then we would tap them out and study the shafts, looking for light streaks. These telltale marks appeared where the shaft came in contact with either the frame or the motor. Such streaks on the shafts indicated poor alignment between the motor and the frame. Sid would polish out the marks, make an adjustment, and try again. He kept at it, saying all along that he wouldn't stop till everything was free, "Like shit going through a goose."

At this point I spent a lot of time just watching my father work to complete this mating structure. Sid loves jobs like this, challenging himself to produce a finished product that is clean and neat, something that will make the guys whistle and call his work "trick."

In the drag-racing world, there are two kinds of go-fast guys: ones who run sloppy and dirty, and ones, like Sid, who run "super sano" (as in sanitized), everything neat and clean and professional. The first kind often resorts to funny fuel to compensate. Sid never raced on anything but straight alcohol because he never felt pushed by his competition to take the risk of blowing up his engine.

With the Vincati, the last critical point of the refit was the engine's countershaft sprocket—it had to sit squarely in line with the rear wheel's sprocket. A misaligned drive train introduces stress as the rear chain chews up the sprocket teeth and itself in the process. But if we had done everything right, then we should have alignment. After an initial inspection with a straight edge and a bubble level, I hooked up a chain.

I gave the wheel a strong spin, and Sid and I watched the chain track straight and true while giving off a pleasing whir. Sid was always captivated by the sight of turning wheels. When we built up a wheel, he would always give it a good spin and time it to judge the freeness of its bearings. As the Vincati's wheel came to a stop, he looked at me and smiled. "My son, we have done it."

With the bridging structure complete, we spot welded all the pieces and removed the straps. For the first time we got a good look at the Vincati. I was amazed. It looked like it came out of a factory, as if all the parts belonged together.

"It should," Sid said, "it's a Colin Sealy frame. When Ducati decided to build the twin, they hired Sealy to do the frame. His dad rode a Vincent. He is British. He made a name for himself by building frames for Matchless. Later he built frames for the Japanese."

"So we are putting a British frame together with a British motor."

"You didn't know that?"

"I guess that's one of your stories that slipped by me. Probably didn't see the relevance then."

"Back when I had the shop, we worked on an early Duke GT. A sailor got it from the factory and brought it back. It was built in 1970, a year before commercial production began, and its frame was stamped number three. The engine was number ten. I never told you that?"

"No."

"This frame and this engine were made to go together," Sid mused. "Just look."

Chapter Twelve

Lucy's Bike

After spot welding the frame, we proceeded to complete the bike in our minds. This is the truth about making a tangible object. As you work, you take its pieces apart and put them back together many times. But in concept, in your mind, you build and rebuild that same object many more times than that. In this process, welding up the frame is a critical step. After that, correcting mistakes often becomes both difficult and expensive.

The Aussie Vincati builders only welded the upper mounts. They considered bolts sufficient for securing the rear plates. Sid, however, prized rigidity, and so on our Vincati the decision was made to extend the welding to those rear plates. Once we were satisfied with our spot welds, we disassembled the bike completely. The frame was then sent off to be professionally welded.

With the frame gone, we had the seat reupholstered and the tank, fenders, and side covers painted. It was while all these pieces were out of our garage and the engine was once again sitting on a dolly that Sid finally broke to me his idea of hopping up the Rapide motor. I should have seen it coming. It made perfect sense: the engine was not needed for the moment and we would have lots of work to do in the interval, building up the chassis, before we needed the motor back. But I balked anyway.

"The motor is fine," I insisted. "We just ran it. You yourself said it sounded great, very low mileage, ready to go." I had spent a lot of time cleaning the motor. I fully expected to bolt it back into the frame upon its swift return. I didn't care that the bike wouldn't be setting any speed records or that it wouldn't look like a show bike. I wanted Sid to ride it.

But Sid found the prospect that his last Vincent engine would be nothing but a lowly Rapide unbearable—even if it came housed in a Vincati. He said, "If I am going to go to all this trouble to build a beautiful Vincati, I want the motor done my way."

And that meant ultratrick, beyond Black Lightning specs. I hesitated because I was nervous about the cost of the additional parts, plus I knew this move introduced a lot of uncertainty. When you take apart a perfectly good, well-running motor, you tempt fate. If the Vincati was going to be Sid's last bike, I wanted to make sure he was out on the road as soon as possible.

Sid, though, was adamant that he wanted to go out in style. So in the end there was just no choice. I went further in hock and bought all the needed internals. But there was another issue. The kind of work he wanted done we couldn't do, not in our bare-bones garage.

This work required a proper machine shop, outfitted with all the right tools and jigs for Vincent work, and it had to be done by a Vincent specialist who does this kind of work every day. In other words, it was a job for a master machinist and that meant Sid's old buddy the Midnight Crew. By the time Sid moved in with me, Sid trusted no one else as much and at this stage of their lives they completed each other's thoughts. So the Crew it was.

While we were preparing to transport the Vincati's engine to Portsmouth, were the Crew worked, I learned from Martha that there was yet another complication stemming from Lucy's operation. The protracted stay in the hospital had left Lucy with a flat head. Weakened from the surgery, Lucy had consistently rested on her back with her head cocked toward her left shoulder.

We had worked on neck exercises to build up enough strength to enable her to hold her head straight, but in the interim all that lying down had caused the back of her head to become partially flat and uneven.

A plastic surgeon told us that Lucy would have to wear a cranial helmet, which would deliver constant pressure to the areas of the skull with which it is in contact. The brain then signals the skull to expand where it does not feel external pressure, and in response the depressed (or flat area) becomes the site of growth, rounding out until it too comes in contact with the helmet. Growth, in other words, follows the path of least resistance.

I knew Lucy, and there was no way this rambunctious baby (then seven months old) would wear a helmet for six to eight hours straight as ordered by the doctor. But I had an advantage—I knew all about wearing a helmet, and the thing about them is that the head retains the sensation of being gripped for some time after you remove it. So instead of strapping it on for six hours straight, I decided to try for twenty to thirty minutes every hour. It also helped that Lucy slept with us because throughout the night I would reposition her so that she learned to sleep on her right side, thus removing pressure from the side that needed to grow.

The final part of my plan was to wear a bicycle helmet whenever we played together. In our favorite game, she would ride on my back while we scampered along as I pretended to be a motorcycle. I did that for thirty-minute stretches and would stop anytime Lucy removed her helmet. This went on for about six months until the beautiful summer day when we got the news from the cosmetic surgeon that we could retire the helmet. As we walked out of the doctor's office, Martha said that I could take credit for Lucy's beautiful head forever.

And so I do.

About a week before Sid and I planned to leave to bring the Vincati motor to the Crew's shop, I got a call from one of Lucy's pediatricians, Denny Cornett. Like me, he was a motorcyclist, and he had just returned from Vintage Motorcycle Days, a popular rally held annually at the Mid-Ohio racetrack, in Lexington, in mid-July. He had bought a Vincent Black Shadow there, and wanted Sid to work on it.

That bike turned out to be the ugliest running example of the breed I have ever seen: broken fins on both jugs, and the rear frame visibly stove in. But it ran. I rode it and came away convinced that mine had been 100 percent straight after my accident because now I knew what it felt like to ride a bent one.

I didn't say anything to Denny at the time, but I was surprised that he had invested in this wreck. It wasn't like you couldn't spot the crash damage. It was obvious. But as we talked I began to understand why he had done it. Denny was such a believer in Sid's ability that he thought my dad could fix anything on two wheels. I had only taken it around the block, but I could sense that the rear wheel was not tracking directly behind the front and that is a formula for having the bike slide out from under you while entering a turn. I crept around the corners and took it up a little past walking speed on the straights, where it stumbled along like a drunk.

After I pulled up from that first ride, I had my doubts that even Sid could tackle this. I hopped off and fell to one knee and really studied the primary drive side of the bike. I saw then that at some point in its history this Shadow had been broadsided by a car. The damage bore the imprint of a steel front bumper, most especially the blow to the rear frame where the tube was flattened and bent inward in a bow. I was terrified that Sid would pass on the job. We needed the money.

The cracked fins could be fixed. The hideous looks could be corrected, and we could get her to run good. But what troubled Sid was the bent rear frame. In the old days, he would have chucked it and put a new one on. But Denny liked the idea of keeping the bike together. And getting a new rear frame member was no longer an easy task— they were hard to come by and extremely expensive.

Fortunately, Sid shared none of this with Denny. We took his down payment and watched him leave.

Then Sid looked at me.

I said, "What the hell hit that?"

"Most likely an old Chevy."

"Do you think it can be fixed?" I said.

Sid thought for a moment. "If anyone can do it, the Crew can. We are just going to have to bring it to him and let him evaluate it."

*   *   *

We got the bike from Denny in late July. My fall semester began mid-August and with it my teaching commitments. Given my schedule, Sid and I agreed that we would have to work fast and tear down Denny's bike so that we could bring the damaged pieces to the Crew when we carried him the Vincati donor motor to hop up. Sid always preferred to have a business reason to make a trip, and now I did, too. Even better, landing this big job—an extensive restoration project—meant that I could get away with doing the Vincati's motor without having to sell the Campbell Rapide, at least not just yet. And that was important to me because I still wanted Sid to have his own Vincent to ride while we finished the Vincati.

Until our Portsmouth trip, the main order of business out in the garage became the near total teardown of Denny's bike. The rear frame member had to be totally stripped. The engine's heads and barrels had to be removed and prepped for the fin repairs.

It quickly became apparent that I would have to do the real grunt work on this job. The hardware had sat for decades, and though there was not a lot of visible rust, separating the parts took tremendous effort. As Sid put it, the metal had lost its memory about how to come undone. Nor did that accident help. That jolt had sent a wave of force through the bike that had bound the threads, and then in the long wait for a set of caring hands, the various metals had begun to flow together. For the first time in his life, Sid just didn't have the strength.

Sid was nervous because all he could do was coach. The last time I had dismantled a Vincent it was my own, and I had almost toppled it in the process. That memory was still fresh in both of our minds. Now I listened to Sid respectfully. Each action had to be a controlled one. You have to sense when you are applying just enough force to succeed without inflicting damage. Sid sat there watching and occasionally bracing the bike while I worked, but it was up to me to "wake up" the nuts and bolts, as Sid called it. Sometimes, a rap with a hammer is enough; if not, you try an air-powered tool. Finally, you grab a propane torch and add heat to the mix.

While I worked, I told Sid that I had come to a decision about the donor motor. "I'll agree to hopping up the Vincati if you make me a promise."

"I'm listening," he said.

"First, you need to know that I am playing a dangerous game of chicken professionally. If I spend too much time out in the garage and lose my tenure, there goes my regular paycheck, plus my benefits, and with Lucy's condition I just can't lose my health insurance. But I also know we can't stop our work out here. So I have to thread the needle and do both: get tenure and be a grease monkey."

"Understood," Sid said in his gravest tone. "What do you want from me?"

"You have to promise me you will stop asking me about what I am writing."

This request surprised Sid. It had been going on for months. When we worked, he continually made me talk about Shakespeare and Milton. I'd been working on a dry tome of literary criticism and for some reason Sid was fascinated by it.

"Look, I never wanted to write this book in the first place," I explained. "But now I have no choice. No book, no job—that's how you get tenure. And when I come out here I just don't want to think about it."

"How can talking about Shakespeare and Milton depress you?" he said. "You always loved books. You always wanted to be a writer—now you are writing a book. How can that be depressing?"

"Because I never wanted to write this kind of book, okay? I wanted to write the great American novel, be the great American writer. Not become some professor who writes incomprehensible criticism that no one wants to read. Look at you. You wanted to set a record at Bonneville. Well, sometimes our dreams don't come true. Just leave me alone when it comes to that stuff and let me do what I have to do."

I looked at him and knew: now he got it.

We pressed on with the teardown of Denny's Shadow. I had successfully removed the upper frame and exposed the motor. Now I needed to back off the nuts that held down the heads and barrels. Everything was covered in a layer of hardened mud.

Increasingly, I began to notice that Sid and I were working with the only sounds in the garage coming from the radio. After I had ruled out talking about books and my job, Sid just didn't know what to say. I was trying to learn how to be less tightly wound. Sid liked to talk and it wasn't fair to force him to work side by side in silence.

Then an idea came to me.

"Why don't we make up a story together?" I said.

"About what?" Sid said.

"A motorcycle. A famous one." Then I added, "And there has to be conflict over it, that's key."

Sid laughed. "You mean something like some guy takes it to the salt flats, sets a record, and then the bike gets stolen."

"Yeah," I said as I began dousing the engine studs in WD-40. It was going to take more than patience and elbow grease to get those nuts to turn. It was going to take Sid's big-ass breaker bar—a socket wrench with a two-foot handle. "Maybe the bike gets stolen several times, like some treasure in a pirate movie."

"You mean a Western," Sid suggested. "A motorcycle is like a cowboy's horse. And it goes from bad guy to bad guy."

"Exactly."

Sid smiled. "Well, I know plenty of stories like that."

And that is how the "book" I took to calling "Buzz Burns and his Fabulous Motor-Cycle" got started. I never wrote down a word but we had found a way to have fun.

With this issue resolved, I really was able to focus much better. In short order I had Denny's bike in pieces.

"You know what you are?" Sid said. "You're a Vincent man now."

When he said it, I was filthy, covered in grime, surrounded by motorcycle parts, and I had the biggest smile on my face.

Then it was time for Portsmouth.

The Midnight Crew's place is a tiny one-bedroom, one-bath, but in back sits his real home: his machine shop. Every dime he made had been plowed into it until it was twice the size of his living quarters. And it had everything: he could bore and hone cylinders, powder coat, bead blast, even plate. And the Crew lived only for the work, lost in all the intricacies of what could be done with metal. I was very fond of him, and we shared a silent bond forged over helping Sid.

As we unloaded the car, the neighbor across the street was on his front lawn pumping out water from his fishing boat before preparing the hull for repair. Beyond that I could see the back of a small church and its parking lot. Much of the housing on the street still wore the surplus green used on military housing, a color common to Tide-water, Virginia. The sight of commercial work going on in front of small bungalows on a beautiful summer morning felt comforting.

The Crew carefully inspected what we brought him, with his jew-eler's glasses resting on his head. He worked rapidly through the pile of Vincent parts until he got to Denny's frame, setting it apart from the rest. He surveyed it for quite some time.

Then he looked at me and Sid and said, "You aren't expecting me to fix that?"

"Don't tell me you can't!" I smiled.

"He should just get a new one."

"It matches the upper frame. He wants to keep them together."

The Crew smiled at the logic of this.

"You can do it," said Sid, "but just remember to record your hours for once." Sid was always frustrated with the Crew about that—the guy would work all day and forget to mark down anything.

"Well, I suppose."

Coming from the Crew, I took this as a definitive yes.

Back in Louisville we collected the Vincati frame from the welder. It looked great. The bridging structure was practically invisible, covered over by the thick, regular beading the welder had introduced into the joints. The black paint swallowed everything so that the frame seemed like one piece.

Sid and I began the task of reassembling the chassis. While I held the rear swingarm in place, Sid drove the pivot tube across and home. He grimaced as if he had just felt a stabbing pain.

"What's wrong?" I asked.

"Some warping," he said tersely. He began to play with the swingarm, moving it up and down as it would on the road. "But it feels free. Nice," he declared a few moments later.

"Warping?"

"It's always a risk when you weld a frame. The intense heat you introduce can cause the metal to alter and then when it cools the frame can sit differently. Let's knock the shaft out, clean, regrease, and reattach the swingarm." Each time we aligned the swingarm with the frame and ran the tube across, Sid grew more satisfied with the action. Finally, he decided to stop.

He said, "We lucked out. The frame is fine."

"So the motor will fit back in?" I asked.

Sid laughed. "We are going to have to wait and find out."

"You don't think . . ."

"Murphy's Law," he said. "It's waiting to get ya."

Sid found the shafts for the top mounting plates and, much to my relief, they slid through easily. We moved on to assembling the front forks. Soon we had both wheels on and we checked alignment. Here too the bike was straight.

"So you think—" I ventured.

"Yes," Sid said. "We lucked out. Let's draw everything up tight and forget about it. Let it sit. It will be fine."

I knew then that I would only get my answer when we brought the motor back and reinstalled it, and that meant I would be waiting a long time. The Crew was not a man to be rushed. From past experience,

I knew it usually took him about a year to do a standard Vincent motor, and this time Sid had asked him for the ultimate. I tried to take comfort in the delay. I thought letting the chassis sit with everything bolted up tight might help correct the slight misalignment I now suspected to be present in the frame.

About a week later, Sid called me over to his side to tell me our pieces were ready to be picked up from the painters. We had instructed the painter to pipe around the tank decal in a square, but he told Sid he had a better idea and Sid told him to trust his instincts. We liked the result very much: it was a delicate black and gold stripe that arced gracefully on both sides of the tank. The side panels were ordered without stripes, but again the painter had continued the striping. The front and rear fenders he left plain, just a beautiful baby blue. The bill set us back another thousand dollars, but it was well worth it.

We had settled on the color after much discussion. We ultimately rejected colors we associated with either the Vincent or the Ducati in the hopes that a neutral color would help bring into focus the Vincati's unique character. Thinking back to the silver Duke, I suggested a metallic gray with gold and black stripes. Sid definitely wanted to go with something understated but he wasn't sold on gray. Then one afternoon we stopped by chance at a local car show, and Sid spotted a classic Corvette painted a rich light blue. "Landell blue" the owner called it. We got back in the car and Sid declared that he knew what color to paint the Vincati.

Once we had the fenders and tank in place, Sid built up the bike's electrical system and finished off its instrument cluster. He decided to retain the original speedometer but he inserted a modern electrical tachometer that would read the motor's revolutions by counting the electrical pulses firing the spark plugs. He also added a British Miller ammeter to enable the rider to monitor the generator and ensure that the system was charging. He retained the stock rear brake but elected to upgrade the front hydraulic system, and in its place we mounted an expensive modern Brembo caliper and master cylinder.

Sid loved to make his own seat, so we spent much time sketching and debating. His aim was to break up the bland, uniform shape of the stock seat, the way he did on the silver Duke. He contoured the seat, giving it a slight rise at the front to help prevent you from sliding up on to the tank when you stop (a "ball blocker" Sid calls it), and then a small but discernable rise midway to mark the rear as the space of the passenger. Finally, he placed a tasteful lip at the far end. When the extra foam was glued in place, we took the seat to Pearson & Marzian to be covered in leather with matching blue piping.

We continued to fiddle with the chassis, mounting turn signals and the rear license-plate bracket, but then real work came to a standstill. Now all we could do was wait until the Midnight Crew was ready for us to come and get the motor. In the meantime the chassis sat, strapped to our assembly bench, with a gaping hole where the absent motor should be.

The body was ready. All that was missing was the heart.

Sid and I filled the downtime by taking rides together. He did some riding on his own as well, usually to a nearby park and back. He rode the Campbell bike around town but only his modern 2000 Suzuki SV650 made him feel comfortable when traveling at speed.

We also did one longer trip. We were thinking of riding to a British bike rally near Cincinnati. When we set off, Sid was apprehensive. He understood that I wanted to ride long distances with him now that I had my Vincent, but he lacked the stamina and the confidence for long riding. His back ached, his knees were weak, and his eyesight wasn't good, especially in dusky conditions. But I found it hard to accept that the man I saw riding the Rattler in those old slides was now seventy-three years old. I promised him that we would turn around whenever he said the word.

We rode north on a pleasant meandering state highway, crossing over into Indiana at the small town of Milton, Kentucky, and then along the Indiana side of the river on a road that snaked past bridge trestles. We stopped for lunch and then crossed over into Ohio while taking a series of wide rolling sweepers leading down into the valley below Cincinnati. The sky ahead was purple with the distinctive fuzzy steaks that signal rain. We stopped for a fill-up and Sid announced that he wanted to turn around.

On the way back, we rolled on Lex and the SV for some side-by-side comparisons. "Level pegging," Sid calls it. We had done this often years ago with his Shadow and the silver Duke. On a clear, straight highway we rode abreast at 100 mph, looked at each other, nodded, and then hit the gas. The SV literally leapt ahead, and in a flash Sid was backing off to cruise at 110 mph. Meanwhile the Vincent lumbered slowly as I watched the speedo tick up to 115 before I managed to catch up. Then I eased off a bit and we were riding side by side at 110 mph. I looked over at Sid, and despite being buffeted by the wind I could see him look at me and nod with satisfaction that I had shown the courage to pull alongside and settle in at 110. As we rode along, he would look over and study my Vincent. I knew he would have some interesting things to say when we got home, but the only thing I could think of then was to hang on and keep up with Sid. We were flying.

Riding fast, we managed to stay ahead of the rain until the very end. At first we rode through a soothing light mist. But then the rain began to fall harder, stinging our faces. Fortunately, I soon spotted a local gas station. We parked under the overhang and sat inside drinking Cokes and watching it pour. We were both hot and soaked. The air around me was heavy with the smell of burnt oil and gas.

"You are going to have your work cut out for you cleaning up the bikes," Sid said.

"No kidding."

"And don't forget to reoil everything."

"I will."

"You know," Sid said, "I'm glad you talked me into going."

We hadn't even made it to the show, but the ride was what mattered.

Later that night, Sid told me he couldn't help but be disappointed with my Vincent's performance. I ribbed him some about not being willing to accept progress. The SV was one the first great superbikes of the twenty-first century. Sid admitted that he might be getting sentimental, but he was convinced that my Shadow could haul ass better than that. To prove it, he had me remove Lex's muffler and hand it to him. Then he shook it. It sounded like a large maraca. Sid's first hunch was confirmed: the baffling inside the pipe was breaking up. Anytime you impede the flow of air out, you fail to achieve optimal performance. That was one big reason my Shadow had fallen behind the SV.

He also didn't like my air filters. Attached to the mouth of the carburetor, air filters prevent dust and dirt from entering into the motor as part of the fuel flow. Mine were very restrictive—and later we would change them, too.

Philip Vincent never liked air filters—he actually sold his machines without them. Vincent maintained that the engine wear introduced from unfiltered carburetors was minimal, and back then he was right. His bikes routinely racked up a quarter million miles without significant engine wear. Now everyone expects filters, and given the current levels of air pollution it is hard not to concede the point. But their use limits performance, especially at the top end on a classic like a big old Vincent. After I removed my filters and changed my exhaust, the transformation was remarkable, but I knew the SV would still walk away from me anytime it wanted to.

And though I hoped my father and I would be able to put our bet to the test, with every ride it became increasingly clear that Sid's knees were failing. He was losing the ability keep himself upright at a stop. He had taken periodic cortisone shots for years, but they were no longer effective. He even tried injections of "animal goop" (replacement cartilage) but they were no help. Now there was no other choice but surgery.

Talking to the doctor about specifics, Sid quickly turned grave.

"Will the surgery mean the end of riding?" he asked.

"Sid, anything's possible," the doctor replied, but his tone told a different story and Sid knew it.

* * *

Lucy's Bike

The next time we went out to work in the garage, both of us knew that the empty chassis was for a bike that Sid would most likely never get to ride. He became convinced that his heart was weak and that the demands of knee surgery would prove too much for him. Now the decision to hop up the motor had come back and bitten him.

While we worked on Denny's Shadow, he would gesture toward the empty frame parked by the wall and ask me, "Do you think we are going to ever finish that one?"

I would answer, "You can't die on me yet: we got too much work to do."

One big issue loomed over us. There was still much machismo among Vincent owners about kick-starting the bike—it's one of life's supreme pleasures. But one backfire can break an artificial knee.

An electric start would set us back close to two grand, but if there was any way at all Sid was ever going to get to ride the Vincati, the bike would need one.

At first Sid balked at the cost. He knew that Martha and I needed to save money for Lucy. For a start, preschool was less than a year away, and art classes and music classes didn't come cheap.

"What am I going to need an electric start for?" Sid said. "I'm finished. Use the money for Lucy. You need to think about her happiness."

But I had promised Sid in the hospital room that we would a build a Vincati for him to ride. I wasn't going to have Lucy grow up living with a grandfather who had no hope. We had to play out this dream, and in a flash I saw how.

"Well then," I said, "Lucy will need it when it's her bike."

Sid looked at me. In that moment the very worst prospect transformed into something wonderful. After that we ordered the kit and were happy to do so, propelled as we were by the thought of Lucy, our own Lady Lightning, riding the Vincati.

Part Four

The Road

Grace isn't often a part of being big.
But on a motorcycle even I became graceful.

—Big Sid

Chapter Thirteen

Last Rides

And then it happened—my book on Shakespeare and Milton was accepted by a publisher, and that meant one thing: tenure. I couldn't have cut it any closer. I had already assembled my binder. For months it had sat like a black stone on my desk while I waited. Then came the day I rode up to the university on my Hawk and slipped in that signed contract. A few days later Sid called me into his room to tell me the Midnight Crew had called and our Vincati motor was ready.

It was quite a week. The summer was ending and school was starting up, but for the first time I felt great. I played with Lucy at our favorite playground and felt certain I would never forget the fun we had racing down parallel slides.

And then it went from good to bad.

After attending a round of kickoff meetings at the university, I came home to talk to Sid about the coming week's schedule. Because fall classes were commencing, I was trying to work out how to juggle things so that I could free up enough time for Sid and I to make a quick dash to Portsmouth and get the Vincati's engine.

I found Sid sitting in his recliner in the dark. I sensed immediately that there was something wrong.

"Reach up there and flip on the light," Sid said glumly.

After I did so, I could see that he looked white in the face.

"Are you okay?" I asked.

"My shoulder hurts."

"The bad one?"

Years ago Sid had fallen in Norfolk and landed on his left shoulder, tearing his rotator cuff. He'd gotten some poor care, and too late, and as a result he had limited mobility with his left arm. For things overhead, he used his right. So why was he in the dark?

"No. My good one."

And then I realized: Sid had fallen a few weeks earlier in the Louisville airport on the way to a Vincent rally in Vancouver. At the time the accident had seemed innocuous enough, and we'd continued on the trip.

"How bad?" I said weakly.

He made a fist and then raised his arm until it was level with his shoulder. Then with a grimace he bent the elbow and pointed his arm up. Then he began struggling to raise the fist toward the ceiling. After a moment he reached over with his other hand, grabbed his bicep, and pushed it straight up. It was the only way he could raise his left arm. And now it was the only way he could raise his right. No wonder he had been sitting in the dark. He could no longer reach the overhead light's pull chain.

"Have you called the doctor?"

"I was waiting to tell you."

* * *

We were there as soon as the office opened. X-rays quickly ruled out the possibility that Sid's problem was the result of a bone break. Unfortunately, that meant that his lack of movement stemmed from a tear in his rotor cuff. To find out, he was scheduled for an MRI, which meant more waiting.

The next Tuesday, I took Sid to Baptist Hospital East. There we met Sid's physician, Dr. Makk, at the MRI station. I sat in the waiting room, holding Sid's watch and the rest of his possessions, while they wheeled him away. Afterward Makk called us into a consultation room.

"It's bad, Sid," he said. "There is nothing I can do."

We sat there in shock.

"Why not?" I asked.

"Well, I could move the muscle around to restore motion so Sid could switch off an overhead light switch, but then he is going to have difficulty picking up a knife and a fork."

"Or wiping my ass," Sid said.

"True," Makk said turning back to my father. "Or using a tool."

Makk thought the best thing to do was to exercise the joint and build up the remaining tendons. Sometimes with work additional motion returns, as you learn how to compensate and swing through the shoulder rotation.

I got up and excused myself.

I was standing outside in the hallway, taking in what we had just learned.

185

Makk came out and found me.

"Matthew, there was nothing you could do."

"It must have happened when he fell in the airport. I shouldn't have taken him on that trip."

"That was just the straw that broke the camel's back. This has been going on for a long time. He has been using his shoulders to offset the knees. It's all the years of hoisting himself up out of chairs that did it. The key thing now is to take action before he loses any more mobility in the upper body. We need to do the first knee now. I'll schedule him for October and then we will do the second as soon as possible."

"We can't do them together?"

"I'll do the first one and then after he recovers I'll do the other."

"How long will he be in the hospital?"

"About a week and then over to rehab. He will probably be home in less than a month. Then you will bring him over here for workout sessions."

"And then when can we do the second knee?"

"Between six months and a year."

I couldn't believe the timing. It was a terrible blow. We were all set to get the Vincati's motor. Now I wasn't making that trip with Sid till he had recovered from his first knee operation.

On the ride home, Sid sat and stared glumly.

As I drove, I thought back to that ill-fated Vancouver trip. I had helped Sid downstairs for the final lineup. The setting couldn't have been more beautiful. The sky was blue with big white clouds and there was a strong breeze. The green mountains, fledged with veins of tan earth, made a sublime backdrop.

I had slung my boots over my back and walked a little on the rough stones strewn along the lakefront. The water was icy cold. I watched my father slowly walk the long line of Vincents, stopping along the way. Despite everything, it was a good memory.

"Can we go get the engine before my surgery?" Sid asked.

"No," I told him. "No more trips. You are going to practice your exercises and get ready for the operation. We have already pushed it too hard."

"You're right," he said.

"We will get it during my spring break in March. We still have to finish painting Denny's bike before winter socks in. We can let the pieces sit and harden, and then when you are over the hump we can start assembling everything."

"Okay," Sid said.

"Then when spring arrives, you will be all patched up and we will bring back the Vincati motor and Denny's parts and launch in."

Now Sid saw the future I was sketching. "We can finish up the Vincati before I go in for my second knee surgery."

"Exactly."

Sid seemed to relax.

"One last thing," he said.

"What?"

"Let's go for some rides, too. Before I go into the hospital."

I looked at him. We had about six weeks before the operation. "Do you feel up to it?" I said.

"Absolutely."

Soon I was teaching again and autumn came to the Ohio valley. All that summer Lucy had continued working with her physical therapist, and the transformation had been a joy to watch. By the time she turned three, it was obvious that this treatment was no longer needed, and for our last session, we went to a public park. The therapist told us that one way to measure a kid's sense of confidence was to watch them wander away from a parent. A kid like Lucy, with a history of trauma, will often walk a few feet from her parents and then feel the need to turn back. But that day, Lucy spotted a group of girls who were much older, perhaps seven or eight, kicking a soccer ball around in the middle of the park. Her eyes lit up and she broke out into an awkward run. She did not look back or stop until she had reached the big girls, one of whom kicked the ball slowly toward Lucy. Lucy lowered her head, charged forward, and gave the ball a big kick straight back.

The next time we had nice weather, Sid and I rode out along the Ohio River, passing the horse farms nestled amid the winding roads that branch off State Highway 42. Out in the country, I hit it hard in third and watched the dial on Lex march right through 80, 90, and 100 to 110. I looked in my rear mirror and watched Sid disappear. Then he came roaring back into view on the SV.

For lunch we stopped at an old country gas station I like, with a few tables and two old pumps with hand levers that you have to flip up. We sat near our bikes and had a sandwich.

"I love that SV," Sid said. "Most guys with a Japanese bike don't get to feel that way—but the SV, it has character. Guys all over the world love it."

"Yeah, I know. How does it compare to the other ones you have owned?"

"Reminds me a lot of my BMW R50, the one I hopped up. That was a back-road burner, too. And Mac's R69, sweet ride."

Last Rides

"I wish I had gotten a chance to ride one of those," I said. "I remember the R90." Sid had only had it for a short time before he sold it back. The owner was an unhinged rich boy who had first offered Sid all his bikes in trade for one Big Sid–prepped Vincent. Sid wanted only the Silver Smoke Boxer and a pile of cash. Soon after, the rich boy bought his bike back but it made for a memorable summer.

I nudged Sid along to his next BMW.

"I always thought your K75S was top heavy. And the engine was just a drone."

"But when you hit the gas, boy did it move."

"Yeah, and even though it was shaft driven, the rear end didn't jack up on you. What about the silver Duke?"

"Ah, that bike was special." He took a sip of his Coke. "Do you remember riding that bike?"

"Sure. I remember one trip where I was following you on the Shadow and I stalled the Duke at a stop sign. You had ridden on. We were just around the corner from the Elizabeth City ferry."

"Right. I rode on board, killed the motor, turned back, and there I saw you by the side of the road, kicking away. But you got it started."

"Yeah," I laughed, "and I made it to the ferry just in time."

For the next ride, I suggested we take out both of the Vincent twins, Lex and the Campbell bike. I really wanted one last ride with us out on Vincent twins.

That day we headed down to Harrod's Bar & Grill on River Road, and I snapped some photos of Sid standing alongside that bike. Even then Sid couldn't resist complaining. He had to remind me once again of the truth: that bike's motor was gutless by Vincent standards.

Putt along at 60 mph and it felt fine, like a late-model Bonny or a mid-size Guzzi, but it had none of that Vincent spunk. If he was a young man, he would tear it all down and rebuild the engine from the gunnels up.

To avoid the complaining, for the next ride I let Sid take out his trusty SV. We pulled off with me in the lead, taking the same route as before, past Harrod's, but then continued on to a one-lane bridge. I was at a standstill there, with one foot down, waiting for an oncoming car to cross, when from behind I heard the wicked snarl of a down-shifting, throttled-shut sport bike. From out of the corner of my eye, I saw Sid running off the road, doing just what he did on the five-mile stretch the day we almost died.

Only now I was the parked car, but this time he didn't have the strength to redirect the bike and he shot off the tarmac at a right an-gle, braking furiously in an effort to stop short of flying off the em-bankment. His rear tire kicked up a rooster tail of drought-parched red Kentucky dirt. I could do nothing but watch and pray he stopped in time. Thank God he did, coming to rest in the mowed grass well short of the edge. I killed Lex's motor and padded over to where he was.

"I forgot about this bridge," he said.

I felt a twinge of guilt for having advanced too far in front of him.

"My fault," I said.

He sat quietly collecting his breath and looking down.

In the silence I felt the heat begin to settle into my riding gear.

At last I asked him, "You ready to roll?"

He restarted his SV and nodded. I kicked Lex to life and pulled away, falling into a much more sedate pace.

I led him up to where River Road reconnects to 42 and then took him out to the old-time gas station diner. On the way I thought about how Sid had said he had forgotten about the bridge even though he had crossed it with me many times—we had ridden across it just two weeks before.

Over lunch I realized that Sid's close call had thrust me back into the geography of our youth. I could see in my mind as never before the landscape when he was young and I was a kid. Old Route 17 and seafood in Elizabeth City. The duck pond where we stopped so often for pictures. Highway 258 in North Carolina and that barbecue stand. Grinding up sugar in old packets while waiting for Sid to come in from inspecting the Shadow. I had wanted to go fishing in the Great Dismal Swamp. But Sid never had any interest. All he wanted to do was ride.

"I can see the old roads," I said.

He nodded.

"When I close my eyes and fall asleep I see them almost every night."

"You know," he said, "at one time the five-mile stretch actually had mile markers that ran from one to five. It was used in tests to license taxi cabs. The signs were handy when you wanted to gauge the accuracy of your speedo."

As we reminisced, the woman behind the counter and her teenage daughter came outside to look at Lex. "Our granddad used to have a Vincent," the girl said. "I wonder if that's it? Could it be?"

It seemed to me that the sight of my bike had taken her back to a better time.

Sid said, "No, that bike came out of Virginia."

"Remember the Vincent engine you did for that truck driver?" I said. It was one of the last jobs Sid had done before leaving Norfolk. That money had paid for his relocation.

"Yes," said Sid.

"Well, that guy lives in Versailles, Kentucky." I turned to the girl and said, "I bet that was your granddad's."

The girl smiled. It didn't matter if I was right. She was back with granddad, on his Vincent.

After lunch I asked Sid if he wanted to ride more, but he was disgusted with himself and depressed about what was happening to him. I didn't push him, because I knew that would only increase the pain.

We turned around and I set a stately pace, keeping Sid in my back mirror. But my mind was still in the past. I remembered when I first rode my Hawk with him that day back in 1994 after I took the bus up from Durham to collect it. Sid took out his Shadow and we headed down to D&D (where he would later buy the SV). He promised the guys there that he would bring them the Shadow to look at.

While on our way, we were stopped at a light and a guy in a pickup truck looked over at the Vincent and shouted, "Hey, is that an antique?"

Without missing a beat, Sid shouted back, "I'm the antique."

Then he engaged first and roared away.

As we pushed on back toward Louisville, more memories came to me: that crazy ride around the Road Atlanta racetrack, unescorted, when Sid hit the back straight on his Shadow and shot ahead. I was behind him on our Vincent Meteor and racked it back wide open and couldn't catch him even though I had passed ninety. A serene late-night ride across Little Five Points in Atlanta and out to Tucker, a "green light run" where we didn't catch one red light the whole way. Runs to Nags Head and Kitty Hawk, Suffolk and Richmond. All the bike nights and all the endless talk, telling guys this was as good as it got, and even though it sounded like a commercial, Sid never tired of saying it. The rides out in the midday sun, taking graceful sweepers along Skyline Drive, from Front Royal down to Asheville. All those times, all of it merging into this one road, under this one sun, burning hard in a sublime blue sky, while on either side of this ribbon of road, the trees flashed by, my father in my mirror, behind me.

Chapter Fourteen

Locked Up

As the day of the knee operation neared, I stopped thinking about stealing any more time for riding with Sid. Nor did he suggest another ride. I guess that after the incident at the bridge he was just too spooked to go out again. Instead he pumped himself up by recounting all the e-mail messages he had received from younger motorcyclists who had gone ahead and done the knee replacements years ago and were still riding. It seemed entirely plausible that he might ride again. Hell, he might even be stronger with the 2.0 hardware installed in his legs.

In the end, the operation itself went well. The anchorages were solid on both ends and the leg was lying good and straight. Now it was going to be up to Sid to fight through the pain and work that new knee.

While Sid was beginning his recuperation in the hospital, I put in my first work sessions out in the garage alone. I decided to keep it simple.

I finished stripping Denny's engine and prepping the pieces for painting. When I launched in, what I discovered was that Vincent black takes a licking, and fifty years of real wear had baked that shit so that no stripper on the shelf would remove it. To do the job, I resorted to air-powered flapwheels. Now my work sessions buzzing down the Vincati's tubes came in handy. I knew the trick would be to remove the paint and just lightly smooth the cases without actually polishing them. You wanted a slightly rough surface to give the paint the best chance to cling and to build up a good coat.

Three weeks after the surgery Sid was back home, and after a day or two of rest, I coaxed him to come out to the garage and see what I had been up to. He was impressed.

He wasn't quite up to working yet, so we just sat and talked till Martha returned from preschool with Lucy. Lucy was old enough now to exhibit great curiosity about the garage and what her Pop Pop and I did out there. So while Sid was in the hospital, I had gone out and bought a toy workbench and had set it up in one corner of the garage, in an area that I had childproofed.

Now Sid got to see Lucy in action out in the garage, banging away at her workbench. She proudly held up her tools and named them: "Screwdriver, hammer, wrench!"

Sid started to sing and Lucy seemed not to mind, or if she did, Lucy now knew that she had the means to make noise of her own.

It was winter. Sid had been home a week or two, and we headed out for another work session. After Sid gingerly made his way into the garage, he turned to me and said, "When are we going to make a trip to Portsmouth?"

I was amazed at his single-mindedness. I said, "It's the middle of November."

Sid's look said, "So what?"

"It's cold," I continued. "There is snow in the mountains and I'm teaching. You need to rehab, and I need to file grades. When we get a spell of good weather, then we will make a run."

I could tell that he still wasn't satisfied. "Look, you can't even lift your leg enough to get it into the car. Let's get you rehabbed at least that far."

"That may never happen," Sid moaned.

"Let's see where you are when I file grades. It's coming up to Thanksgiving already. I promised Martha we would have a nice holiday."

Over the next few weeks, we reassembled Denny's lower end: the primary drive, the timing chest, and the gear change/kick start internals. We were getting everything ready for doing the top end: putting on the pistons and then slipping on the cylinders and heads. I knew Sid was eager to get to that point because then we would have to go to Portsmouth.

As Sid and I resumed our regular work pattern, I put on the audiobook of Boswell's *Life of Johnson*, something I'd been playing while Sid was in the hospital. Sid was delighted to listen to it while we worked. He loved the image of Samuel Johnson that emerges in that account, and recognized him as a kindred spirit: a big lovable oaf who was curious about the world and everything in it.

As I told Sid more about Johnson, I realized something else had changed: I was suddenly willing to talk about what I did as a professor. I had proved to myself that I could do good work in the garage. If Sid wanted to know what I thought about books, I would tell him. This pleased Sid, because he never went to college. The only time he sat in a college classroom was when I was at Duke and I took him to the first class of the semester, on, of all things, medieval English drama. The other students had projected the normal affect that this was just another day in school, but not Sid. He looked like Lucy did when I took her to the Louisville Zoo and she stood before their antique merry-go-round for the first time.

And though I was struck then by his look of pure joy, I had been so caught up in my own terror of failure that I had denied my dad a gift I could have given so easily for so long. But now all that resistance had vanished. I answered all his questions and talked about the books I loved and what it was like to go to college. Finally, he felt comfortable asking me how I thought he would have done.

"Just fine," I said. "You really would have done just fine."

Hearing that, Sid looked both astonished and relieved.

While we listened to Boswell, we built up the various subassemblies of Denny's Vincent. It was slow work. It took a lot of effort to shim all the moving parts. When you build up a Vincent's timing chest you often add thin washers (shims) or resort to other tricks to make sure the parts have sufficient free play for near-frictionless movement. Where before I would have insisted that I take the lead, I was now content to watch Sid and provide a second pair of eyes. I hunted for the overlooked issue, the obstruction or excessive play still present in the system. The arrangement made for satisfying work.

Time passed in the garage and out. Soon I had filed grades for the fall semester, and Sid was finally able to get himself into the car to the point where we felt confident about driving to Portsmouth to get the engine.

Locked Up

We began watching the weather, looking to see when a warming pattern might settle in over the mid-Atlantic. I hated the thought of making the trip during icy conditions because I was still afraid Sid might slip and injure himself. Finally, right after the New Year of 2004, we got a stretch of abnormal temperatures, a good ten degrees warmer than usual.

I sat down with Martha and told her I thought it was time to make a quick trip with Sid to Portsmouth to get the Vincati motor and Denny's parts. We had celebrated Thanksgiving, Hanukkah, and New Year's together, and now it was time to get this out of the way.

"Another trip?" Just two words and then silence. Her face said it all: she didn't want me to go.

"Look, I don't want to go either. But . . ." I didn't think I needed to finish the thought.

"I know, it's about the paying jobs," she said with a frown.

"We need to finish Denny's bike and get on to the next one." I could have said more, but she and I had gone over the bind we were caught in again and again.

Money.

The university was about to grant me tenure, but that was little comfort to Martha. Six years after our move, she was still living the life of an adjunct instructor of creative writing. She got dirt pay and no benefits. But she wanted to teach and live as a poet, and the only way we could make that happen was for me to work with Sid out in the garage.

I tried hard to get Martha to see that her anger at the university was shading over into bitterness toward me and Sid. Now, as I prepared to hit the road, I feared I would be coming back to a major problem at home. It wasn't just the three days away; it was the recognition of what was to follow. Martha knew already that Sid and I would be out in the garage working around the clock on the Vincati, racing to finish it up before the second knee operation.

But as I told her I loved her and would do what I could to ease the burdens we both faced, I did not know if such words would be enough to compensate for how she felt whenever she set foot on the campus of the University of Louisville. Because every time she did so, the world told her what it really thought of her and her poetry: twenty-five hundred bucks a class, with no benefits, and no job security. I could do nothing to change that.

By now I knew the route to Portsmouth like the back of my hand. And I also knew to knock on the Crew's workshop window rather than his house's front door.

The Crew had always looked older than Sid despite being a few years younger—but I was shocked to find that wasn't the case anymore. When Sid hobbled in, I caught the Crew's eye. His face remained set in its characteristic mask of calm indifference, but we locked gazes and I could see a flicker.

The Crew quickly found a tall stool for Sid. There on the bench to the right of us sat the Vincati motor, though it was hidden under an old white bedsheet. Sid sat down, and after a few moments of incidental banter, he noticed the covered engine.

"That's the Vincati motor, isn't it?"

The Crew nodded and smiled slightly. It was as emotional as he got.

Sid looked at the sheet and then said, "Whenever you're ready. Let's get the show on the road!"

Never before had I seen the Crew resort to theatrics. But in this instance it was appropriate. With one motion, he grabbed the sheet and lifted it off, and there in front of us sat the most stunning Vincent motor either of us had ever seen: a real jewel, with no trick of presentation held back. The covers gleamed like chrome even though they were only polished aluminum. The engine crankcases were a restrained gray satin sheen.

Sid was blown away. "My God. It should be in a museum." He hobbled over to study it closely. "Some purists would pronounce it 'over-restored.' I say, fuck 'em!" And he laughed.

"But it's not over-restored," I insisted. "It doesn't cross the line. Irving would have approved."

At the first Shadow Lake Rally, Sid had witnessed Phil Irving berate an unsuspecting owner for tarting up his Vincent, dispatching him with the quip: "You have ruined my motor!" For Sid the line is drawn at the level of polish given to the crankcases. And the Crew had indeed walked that fine line, going with the gray satin sheen finish. But he had stopped just short of a true chrome polish, a look that Sid equates with a street whore.

"It's incredible," I said, "but once we get her on the road, it is not going to look over-restored."

The Crew caught my eye and accepted the compliment. It was as if he lived in a world of metal, which, after all, is really a slow-moving liquid. Slow down time enough and you can see metal moving. In order to bond with the Crew you have to be able to enter this alternate mode of being—the one where immense forces register on the surface in the slightest of alterations.

I pointed to the nice spot of black he added to the timing cover to make the raised and unpainted letters that spell "Vincent" pop. I spotted the flashes of bronze hardware he had added. This got a nod and the trace of a smile from the Crew.

Sid and I couldn't pay the Crew for his work, so I thought the prospect of celebrity might afford some compensation. Accordingly, I had promised the Crew that we would get this bike in the pages of *Cycle World*.

But over lunch that afternoon, I learned he had a problem with this idea.

"Don't use my real name," Crew said. "I got enough work as it is."

"Well, what should I call you?"

He thought about it a moment. "In the navy we used to talk about the Midnight Crew."

"And if I honor that request, it's okay to show off the bike?"

The nod of his head was almost imperceptible.

When we got back to Louisville, I walked into our house through Sid's side and tried to surprise Lucy. She was sitting on Martha's lap, watching a baby video. I crept over to the couch and stood behind them. I kissed Martha on the head. Sensing my presence, Lucy turned and looked at me and said excitedly, "Daddy!"

But then she immediately went back to watching *Baby Songs*, ignoring me.

I looked over at Martha, who till then had not acknowledged my presence. She whispered, "She is angry at you for going away. Give her time."

Locked Up

The next afternoon Lucy's mood remained icy. I was convinced that Lucy was once again channeling her mother's anger. So to patch things up, I took my daughter out to the garage.

I have spent a fair amount of time watching kids play on motor-cycles, and like most Vincent owners, I let my friends pose their kids on my bikes. You can tell instantly which ones take to it.

I set Lucy on my Honda Hawk GT. Her eyes lit up as she reached for the controls and she was off, blasting down some road in the countryside.

Then in late January, on a warm Saturday afternoon, Sid and I went out to the garage with the intent of finally finishing the job.

That afternoon I rocked the motor first one way and then the other while Sid slid two jacks underneath. Then while he sat on one side steadying everything, I began cranking the engine up to return it to where it had sat over a year ago. So much had happened in the inter-vening months: back then I had no idea if I was going to get tenure, Lucy was just learning how to walk, and Sid was still hobbling on two bad knees.

Soon the front head found its way between the frame's pair of front bracket plates. We slid the shaft through and it aligned with little ef-fort.

Sid was confident that it was now just a matter of jacking up the rear of the motor and it would enter the back of the frame. The rear cylinder head would then find its home just as the front had. As I worked the jacks, I watched the rear of the motor rise. It entered the frame. I tried to remain calm. Things were going as planned. We had done everything right. I worked the jacks some more and noted that the rear cylinder had entered its moorings as well. Now Sid was sighting the three remaining sets of holes and waiting for them to align.

"Keep it coming," he said.

In a moment I saw that the entire chassis was rising and the tie-down straps we had securing the bike were growing taut.

I stopped. "It's locking up."

"Yeah. Let's lower and repeat."

We did but we got the same result. I played some with rocking the bike in an attempt to get the motor to spring a bit upward and perhaps settle into alignment. We noticed that these repeated efforts were inching the bike forward to where it might rock off its center stand, taking the motor off the jacks with it. It didn't take much to imagine the whole thing crashing to the floor.

"You don't think it's warped?"

Sid just looked at me. "Let's get it back out, and in the morning we will scrape the paint off the inside of the frame. Then we can see where it is striking."

"It can't be much," I insisted. "We got one shaft and the other three are damn close." The three sets of holes where overlapping, each by about half, revealing oblong shafts of light running through the machine. But as it was now, try as we might, we could not get the motor to swing forward and up the remaining distance to get those holes to open up.

"Close don't count," Sid said. "Let's stop for now."

I told Martha we were knocking off early and suggested that she get Lucy so the three of us could go stroll around the neighborhood.

When we got in front of the garage, Lucy said, "You know what's in there?"

"What?" I said, playing along.

"Junk!" Lucy jumped up and down while she said it.

I looked at Martha, whose sense of humor had been adopted by our daughter. Sid burst out in a belly laugh, and I scooped up Lucy and spun her around in celebration of her comic brilliance. For a long time after, Lucy was prodded by her Pop Pop to repeat that punch line whenever the time was right.

Junk.

The next morning we went out early. I scraped the paint off every interior surface of the frame and then sanded and scrubbed it all down for good measure. Then we tried again and got the same result. Now Sid had me clean the surfaces again, and this time he added black marker to the motor's surfaces to allow us to see where the engine was hitting. We repeated the process: the motor went up, the same three holes failed to align. We lowered it again and now we examined the engine to determine where it was striking. Sure enough there was scraping through the black ink that revealed the bright aluminum cast surface of the rear swingarm pivot lug.

Here it helps to know a little more about a Vincent motor. The bottom half is called the crankcase and it is comprised of two matched pieces, a left and a right, that are bolted together by studs that run horizontally. The front of the crankcase is symmetrical but the rear is not. The left side is longer, extending straight back beyond the clutch housing where it accepts the swingarm pivot shaft. This shape is not matched by the right crankcase. That piece ends earlier and sweeps in to expose the front drive sprocket around which the rear chain runs, so it can turn the back wheel of the bike. Sid had spotted gouging on

the longer left-hand side and now wanted to lay a flat file on that surface and reduce it by a few thousandths of an inch.

I didn't want to do that. "I don't want to scar up that jewel. Think
of the Crew's work."

"It's just a little richness. You can't even see it. It's purely cosmetic."

But I wanted to know where it was striking on the frame. "Let's
figure exactly what the problem is," I insisted. "We know where it is
striking on the engine. Let's figure out how to leave a telltale on the
frame."

Sid said, "Wite-Out correction fluid on the motor. We rack it up
and look at the streaks the contact leaves."

"We'll go tomorrow and get some. Now I have to teach," I said.
"Let's call it quits."

Day two without progress. I was starting to get spooked.

On Tuesday morning I got up ready to go out into the garage. In the
den, on the way over to Sid's side of the house, I discovered Martha
packing while Lucy was watching TV.

"What are you doing?" I asked.

"I can't take it anymore," Martha said. "You spend all your time
out in that garage. You're distant and distracted. It's like nothing else
matters. It's not healthy. Not for me. Not for Lucy."

I was dumfounded.

"Where are you going?"

"Hawthorn Suites."

"A hotel?"

"Lucy likes hotels. We'll swim, relax. Go somewhere where we
don't have to be around you."

I had no idea what to say.

"Are you coming back?"

"At some point. Though . . ."

"You mean, if you could you would leave."

"Matthew, you've changed."

I nodded my head. I looked over at Lucy. It appeared as if she wasn't listening. She was three. I wondered how much of this discussion she was taking in. Sadly, I knew the answer.

What was I doing? How had it come to this? I couldn't blame them for leaving.

"Go ahead and go," I said. "Call and leave the number. We'll talk tonight."

I walked outside to find Sid sitting on his stool, staring at the Vincati. Martha and Lucy walked out past us to the car, but Lucy broke away from her mother and ran into the garage.

"Lucy, no!" Martha yelled. She insisted that she was afraid for Lucy because the garage was a dangerous space, filled with chemicals and tools.

"Bye, Pop Pop," Lucy said.

"Have fun with your mommy," he said automatically. Normally, he would have talked to her more, but he was lost in thought about the Vincati. Like father, like son.

I washed my hands and then picked Lucy up, holding her tightly and nuzzling her neck, breathing in her sweet smell.

"I love you more than anyone and anything in the whole world."

"You always say that, Daddy."

"I know I do. You are so smart. Have fun with Mommy."

* * *

And then they were gone. My head was spinning. But I had seen it coming. Sid, of course, was oblivious, which was a good thing—I didn't want him to know what was going on in my marriage. Regardless of how I felt about Martha going, I knew we couldn't leave the bike half-finished—there was no choice but to dive back into it.

She was right. Sometimes it was like nothing else matters.

So we painted the sides of the engine white. We cranked it up until everything lodged and then we lowered the engine back out. The interior of the frame was left a solid white. We learned nothing.

After we cleaned up our mess, Sid begged me again to let him file a little and see if there was improvement. I gave in but insisted we repeat what we had just done so that he had a fresh set of marks. He agreed to only file until the marks were smoothed away and we would refit. So we cleaned and repeated and once again raised and lowered the motor so that Sid had fresh marks. After a prayer and an apology to Irving, he worked the metal until he was satisfied. Then we tried again with no improvement. We lowered the engine back out and again there were identical marks.

Sid wanted to file some more. I said no. We still didn't know for certain why the motor was not going all the way, and I was not going to continue to guess at a solution. Usually, I was no purist, but I just didn't want to alter our motor without being certain it would solve the problem.

My mind was going in circles: it's bent. It can't be bent. It's bent. What did G say, they fuck up the frame? It's bent. It can't be bent. In desperation, I cried out, "What are we gonna do?"

Sid had reached the end of his rope. "Get a Dumpster," he said.

It was just a joke but given what was going on with Martha, I was in no laughing mood. I had sacrificed so much and the only thing he could hold out to me was a bad joke.

"You know," I began, "when I was a kid, you could never teach me anything. What I learned about motorcycles I learned on my own and from Stan. This is the one thing I thought you were good at, and your answer is 'get a Dumpster.'"

He took in my words and grew quiet.

"Yeah, well I may have been a bad father," he said, his voice just above a whisper. "But you could have had worse."

Sid's father had beaten him mercilessly and he bore those scars for life. But I wasn't going to let him hide behind it.

"Why didn't you stand up to him? Why didn't you protect your mother? Why didn't you do something?"

"I couldn't. I guess I don't have in me what you have in you. Even though I hated him, I could never stand up to him. He just got to me." He dropped his head and clearly didn't want to talk anymore.

But I was having none of it.

"So you knew what he had done to your mother. I was just a child and even I knew there was something really wrong with that woman. He destroyed her mind. She was like a child, like Lucy."

By now Sid was sobbing.

"She was so broken," he whispered.

Sid wouldn't look at me or say anything more. I watched him sit there and rock on his stool.

I started for the door; then I stopped. I couldn't leave because Sid would need help getting up. I turned, ready to tell him what I really thought, once and for all.

"Don't you get it? He didn't just take control of her, he took control of you. Right down to your fucking dreams. You should have listened to Bugs and gone to college."

I laid my hand on Lex's throttle and looked at it as if I expected this Vincent that had once carried Bugs to back me up. "He got so far into your head. Don't you know why you never went to Bonneville? It was never my mother. It was him."

At that he looked up and I saw a face set in a mask of utter terror. I had taken away what had been the one refuge Sid thought he had from his father. Motorcycles had always been his escape, but even they weren't outside the scope of his old man's reach. I had nothing else to say so I took a stride toward him. Then I remembered my grandfather, and the wicked smile he flashed after insulting me on my birthday all those years ago.

And so my life ran parallel to Sid's. He had wanted to truck the Rattler out to Bonneville and with Paul or another buddy in the saddle they would have broken Rollie's record. Me? I was going to write the great American novel.

Instead, I was beating up my old man in the garage. My wife and kid had gone. I was going broke.

And none of that was Sid's fault.

My anger had finally broken. I sat down and waited for Sid to stop crying.

"I'm sorry," I said.

Once he collected himself, I added, "You must be hungry."

"Yeah. I'm hungry."

I helped him inside.

"You eat," I said. "I'm going for a ride."

* * *

Locked Up

At the Hawthorn Suites I found Lucy and Martha in the pool. They had the place to themselves. Lucy had a bunch of waterwheels and buckets set up all over the steps leading down to the shallow end. She didn't see me and I watched her play. Then I took a seat near Martha and stared at our reflections trembling on the pool's surface.

"Did you solve your problem?" Martha said without looking up, her eyes trained on Lucy.

"No."

At that Lucy looked up and realized I was there. Her face filled with joy. "It's Daddy!"

"How long are you going to stay?" I asked Martha.

"I don't know."

She turned away and watched Lucy.

"Listen," I said, "You are right. I love you. I love Lucy. I can rein it in."

Martha laughed, but it was clear she didn't find anything funny.

"Go home and keep working. I don't want to go home to that insanity. Everything in that house revolves around one thing: what's wrong in the garage."

I knew she was right. I would only set us up for failure if I had her come back and then couldn't stop. I had to solve this Vincati problem before I could fix anything else.

The garage was still empty when I got back. I walked over to the Vincati and sat alongside it. It was an object. Nothing but an object. How had I let it take possession of me? But I was kidding myself by asking the question. It hadn't taken possession of me. I had always been its possession.

It was then that I realized that maybe the white paint test had told us something after all—that it wasn't a problem with the sides. Maybe it was a problem with the motor's rear left edge. I walked over and began to raise the motor and as I cranked the jack I studied the far back of the engine just as it met the rear of the frame. I grabbed the motor and pushed up, feeling it just make contact with the frame, and as I pushed again and again I realized that the motor was cocking. It was hitting resistance up top that was twisting the bottom slightly to one side before rising. I lowered the motor down and looked up. It was the added mounting plate, the one on the left side of the frame. The welder had laid a good-looking bead on the inside, but it was too rich. That curve of added bead was crowding the motor's rear edge.

That was it!

And what this meant was that we didn't need to file the side of the motor. We needed to round its edge. I raced inside and walked Sid through my hypothesis.

"Could it be so simple?" he wondered.

"Let's test it. Let's put white paint on just the motor's edge." We did, and this time when we cranked it up I didn't crank all the way but just to that point where I first hit resistance. Then I lowered it and there was paint on the first bead of weld.

"You're right," Sid said.

"How could we have been so stupid as not to spot that?"

"Who cares?" Sid was genuinely happy that I had solved something that had beaten him.

"You want to do it?" Sid held up the file.

"Oh, no. And have Irving's ghost haunt me for the rest of my life? You have the touch. I'll work on the frame."

Sid laughed. "That is hard-assed steel."

Locked Up

I started with emery cloth but then quickly gave up. It truly was hard steel and rubbing it wasn't going to do anything. I resorted to the high-speed grinder and a pink-tipped mounted stone. The work involved lying on my back in a contortion that Sid could never have done. After I exhausted this effort, Sid offered up a few more prayers for forgiveness and lightly filed, rounding off the motor's edge. We stopped and repeated the procedure and this time we made considerable progress. The oblong ovals were now much closer to round. We lowered and repeated. Now we watched as the rear cylinder head came into alignment. That left only the two shafts going through the rear of the motor. We lowered once more. The rear engine mount is designed to be a loose fit, in order to accommodate the engine expansion that comes when the Vincent's aluminum motor gets hot and grows in length.

"Let's give the rear head some more play," Sid said. It looked like it needed some and that would also help allow the engine to nestle better with some room to float.

I fired up the air compressor and brought over the air grinder and the right mounted stones and watched while Sid further opened up the holes in the mounting brackets through which the rear cylinder head gets secured.

Sid's bracing system in the rear was more complex than what the Australians, the only others to do what we were trying, were running. Like us, they employed two shafts to secure the engine's base: the swingarm shaft and the one from which the Vincent hung its footrests. But Sid had also decided to sleeve both shafts. Made by the Crew, these sleeves were designed to fit snugly within the frame. Then when you drew up the nuts, the sleeves would work to resist the inner crush, thus preventing distortion or bending. Now we were just shy of getting those sleeved shafts in place.

Once Sid was done working on the rear cylinder mounting brackets, we cleaned the area and began cranking the motor back into position. The rear cylinder shaft aligned and we ran it through.

"Now try the footrest hanger," Sid said.

I pushed it in with my hands and tapped it with a mallet. "It's coming!" Sid said. "Now try the swingarm shaft."

I started the last shaft by hand and began driving it across.

Tap tap tap tap dunk.

"Whoa," Sid said. "That is damn close. Take a look."

I walked around and saw that the tapered end of the shaft was emerging but the rear mounting plate was hitting the front half of the threads where the shaft thickened to its full size. You could drive it across but it would scar up the threads. I once again crawled under the bike and stared at where the bead had been striking the engine. I felt around with a feeler gauge and studied the surface. "It looks free to me."

"Aw," Sid said, "three shafts in and the last one, closest to the weld, is showing the slightest misalignment. That's nothing. You could actually drive the shaft across but you want everything to float free, you don't want to introduce a point of locked-up stress," Sid said. He had had enough of raising and lowering the motor.

"Fire up the air compressor," he said. "Let's just open up the exit hole slightly and the shaft will emerge, pretty as pie."

"It won't compromise handling?"

"I don't think so. What I need to do is very slight, and when we draw up the shafts so that all the flats are kissing, the frame and the motor will straighten out as they come to live together."

I shrugged. "Let's do it."

Finally, after a few light strokes, Sid stopped. I walked around to the other side of the bike. "Ready?" Sid nodded. I tapped the shaft with a mallet. I didn't hear any contact so I kept knocking it forward.

"Whoa," Sid said and smiled. I saw the shaft get pushed back toward me. From the other side Sid was working it and it moved freely. All four shafts were sitting nice and pretty.

"Remove the jacks," Sid said.

Motor and frame were united. Those five words couldn't measure up to what we'd managed to do.

Chapter Fifteen

First Start

I couldn't quite believe we'd fixed this, the biggest challenge we'd faced. I called the hotel with the hope that Martha would be overjoyed, but I was being naive.

"I'm happy for you. I guess," Martha said. "But Matthew, there will be another problem, and another part, and another crisis. It never stops."

"No," I said, "it stops now."

"What? You aren't going to finish the bike?"

"No, I mean I'm going to change. I'll do whatever it takes. I'll limit the time I spend out in the garage. I don't want to lose you."

A long pause.

"Okay, you think about how that's going to work."

"I will."

More silence. Then I said, "You aren't coming home?"

"Lucy's already asleep."

"Okay, I understand."

"Good night, Matthew," my wife said.

* * *

The next morning Sid and I decided to take a breather for a few days. The work had taken its toll on both of us, plus I had a bigger issue to face.

I called Martha and told her that I would not go out into the garage for the rest of the week. We would relax and make an effort to reconnect.

"I love you, Martha," I said.

"I love you. We're on our way."

Finally, they were home.

It was great to be able to tell Martha to spend the rest of the day working on her poetry—Lucy and I were headed downstairs to the playroom. We had some catching up to do, too.

Once I'd set up Lucy's princess tent, she told me that she had invented a game and she wanted me to guess what it was.

She began to carry her toys into the tent: her blocks, stuffed animals, dolls.

"Do you know what the game is?"

"No, Lucy, I don't."

Then she climbed into the tent. She stuck her head out and said, "It's called garage."

As we played peekaboo, I was struck with the realization that all the trauma Lucy had from the heart surgery was finally gone.

Here at last was a happy Lucy, home, along with her mother, thank God.

*   *   *

Next day, with Lucy at preschool and Martha writing, Sid announced he wanted to go for a ride.

"Just a short one. Around the neighborhood," he said.

"Okay," I said. "Let's pull out a bike and see how you do."

I had no idea if Sid was ready and I was scared.

"Which bike?" I asked.

"The Campbell bike."

I rolled it out.

He said, "Start it."

After I got it running, I hopped off and held it by the front forks while he got on. He gunned the throttle a few times. Then he looked over at me and smiled. He engaged first and pulled off, making a graceful left-hand turn out of the drive toward the stop sign at the end of the block. I watched him slow as he approached it then make a slow, coasting right-hand turn. I heard the bike shift into second and then it disappeared.

A moment later I wondered why I couldn't hear the Rapide anymore. I walked to the end of the block and spotted the bike toppled over at the next corner at the stop sign. He must have tried to put his feet down.

Sid was on the ground, still in the riding position, pinned under the bike. I ran toward him, calling, "Dad! Are you okay?"

"Goddamn it!" I heard him yelling. "Get this thing off me!"

"Give me a second," I said. Righting a bike is tricky business. You can destroy your back if you lift the wrong way. Sid's right leg was trapped, with his calf pinned between the exhaust pipe and the asphalt.

I circled the bike and took up a squatting position on the right side, so that instead of trying to pull the bike up with my hands, I would push up against the forks to get just enough lift for Sid to wiggle his leg free. I pushed with my legs and felt the bike lift every so slightly.

Sid announced, "I'm free."

Now Sid was able to reposition himself and crawl backward off the bike. "Get her up!" he pleaded. For Sid there was nothing more shameful than to see his bike on its side. I righted the bike and put it on its side stand.

"How am I going to get up?" he said, his voice quaking. I looked at him.

I returned with a chair from the garage. I placed the seat in front of him. And while I lifted by his belt, he pushed up off the chair until we got him standing.

"Can you walk?"

"I think so. Get my cane." He stood with his hands on the chair.

We walked back to the garage, and I got him sitting on his stool. Then I ran back to the corner and walked the bike home.

When I rolled it into the garage, Sid was crying.

I put the bike on its rear stand.

By the time I returned with the chair, he had collected himself. "Did I hurt it?"

"Fuck the bike," I said. "Are you okay? How is your knee?"

"It's fine. Do you see any damage?"

I knew he needed to know. The front exhaust had a little gravel rash and the gearshift lever was bent. But levers are easily straightened; Sid had done it for me many times. And as for the long lower exhaust pipe—a little semichrome combined with some running to bronze the freshly scarred area and she would look as good as new.

The fact that the blow fell largely on Sid's leg had prevented the bike from any real harm.

I grabbed a towel and started wiping down the tank from where the gas had run out while the bike had been on its side.

As for Sid, I could see that the palm of his hand was cut up and his calf had a nasty burn from the exhaust pipe. But if we kept the wounds clean and he remained active, I thought they would heal up. He walked fine and was insisting that his knee felt okay.

Once I'd gotten Lucy from preschool, Sid sat in his recliner. He hid his anxiety and let Lucy jump up into his lap to play. Watching them I convinced myself that Martha would never have to know.

Lucy was learning her alphabet and loved to show Pop Pop all the letters she could now draw, both upper- and lowercase.

"Lets all draw!" Lucy said. She liked to play the teacher now.

Pop Pop drew. A motorcycle, of course. I did one, too, but his was better. He was quite a good freehand draftsman. I remember him doing it back when I was a kid. Then he sat for a while and drew an intricate small bottle. He wrote Chanel No. 5 on it and added a puffer attachment at the bottle's top. He held it up to Lucy.

"It's a perfume bottle!" Lucy said.

"Why did you draw that?" I asked him.

Sid told me how when his mother died, he had found an empty bottle of Chanel No. 5 he had once given her in her top dresser drawer. After he visited Stevenage, he had flown back to Germany via Paris, and there he had bought the Chanel as his one big gift for his mother from his hitch in Europe. The seal had never been broken, so she had never used it. It had just evaporated over time.

221

When Martha came home, she noticed the scrapes on Sid's hand and the red burn on his leg, and asked about them. Sid told her he stumbled walking out to the garage and scraped himself against the cinderblock wall. She accepted the story and turned her attention to Lucy who was turning expert somersaults across Pop Pop's couch.

The next afternoon, I was eager to get back to the Vincati, but when I asked if Sid wanted to work he declined, saying he didn't feel up to it. And so it went for the next few days. Given that I was trying to limit time in the garage, anyway, I let it go.

I understood why Sid had wanted to go for a ride on the day he fell—he was all pumped up from having finally gotten the Vincati's motor into its frame. So was I. But I couldn't help feeling that I should have stopped him. He was exhausted from all the hard work in the garage. He was still weak from the surgery but didn't even try the much lighter SV, on which he was more comfortable.

Now it seemed that instead of finishing work on the Vincati, Sid was falling into a deep depression. Understandably, the accident highlighted his mortality and the loss of the thing he loved most—going for rides.

After a few days, Martha started to notice the change in Sid, too.

"What is wrong with him?" she said. "I've never seen him like this."

"Like what?"

"You know. Even Lucy knows. He's not himself."

I looked at her. Again and again, we had found Lucy sitting on the edge of Sid's bed with him lying prone on it, staring up at the ceiling. "Don't be sad, Pop Pop," she would repeat.

"He's depressed."

"Is this because of me?" Martha said. "Because if it is, I can't take that."

"What do you mean?"

"I asked for some sanity in this house. I asked for some psychic space of my own. I didn't demand that you stop working in the garage. I am not going to be the reason he sits around all day and mopes."

"That's not it," I said.

I didn't blame her for taking Sid's misery personally, but I still didn't want to tell her that he had dropped a bike. On some level I held out hope that he just might ride again.

But I realized that I had to come clean. It wasn't fair to punish Martha by making her feel that the black cloud that had descended over the house was all her doing.

She was shocked when I told her about the ride and the accident and wanted to talk to Sid, but I begged her to say nothing. I had promised him that it was a secret. Besides, Sid had made the decision: that was the last ride. Bringing it up now would only make things worse.

"So what are we going to do?" Martha said.

"Let's just see if he snaps out of it."

February turned to March, and though I could get Sid to walk up and down the street to rehab, he wouldn't go near the garage.

When I learned that my tenure decision had finally gone through, complete with the president's signature, not even that cheered him up. At the University of Louisville, as at most American universities, the granting of tenure entitles the professor to petition for a paid release from one semester of teaching. Well, I promptly entered my request, and when I got that additional bit of good news, I once again played it up to Sid: in just a few weeks time, I told him, I would be filing grades and then he and I would have a full six months, from May to mid-January, to finish the Vincati.

"Yeah," he said, blandly, "great. Congratulations." There was no fire in him.

I decided to try a practical approach. I reminded him that the weather was getting nice and we had promised Denny his bike would be ready to ride. We hadn't even attached the pistons, let alone finished the motor or reassembled the chassis, and we had taken a lot of his money and wanted more. We had to get back to work.

"You're right," Sid said. "I'm acting like a child."

"Or I'm gonna fire your ass!"

This attempt at humor seemed to lift him, a bit. We'd see if it would last.

The next day we went out to the garage to reacquaint ourselves with Denny's Shadow. I had never replaced pistons. It's a complicated task—and I was eager to learn. The Crew had replaced the cylinder liners because they were worn beyond original specs, but it was left to us to hone the bores. I attached a tool Sid called a Christmas tree to our handheld drill. Resembling a circular brush, this attachment has hundreds of carbide balls on individual spring steel wires. Next I inserted the drill's business end into the mouth of the cylinder and spun it slowly up and down to get good crosshatching on the inner walls. This action helps the piston's rings and the cylinder wall to seal (or "seat"). Of course, all components are then washed in hot soapy water to flush out the "swarf" inevitably left behind from this procedure. Then, after mak-

224

ing sure that the piston has about 4 thou of an inch clearance between it and the cylinder in which it will live, you add the three rings to it. Each ring is made with a gap so that when squeezed by the cylinder wall its two ends can't meet and lock up—if they do, they break. You want about 16 thou of an end gap. Then you have to mount the piston on the end of its rod and secure it with a gudgeon pin. The tricky part comes with adding the two circlips to keep the pin locked in place and unable to slide out from either side.

I was hoping that as we worked Sid's mood would improve, but it didn't.

"You have got to snap out of it!" I said.

"I can't. At some point a man realizes he is finished."

"But we have to finish Lucy's bike." No effect. I looked at his shattered face and we were back in the hospital right after the heart attack.

"Yeah," he finally said. "I'll get on it right away, Mr. Boss Man."

In frustration, I pointed at the Vincati. "I want to take Lucy for rides on that. Just like you took me."

Sid turned away to wash his hands, collected his cane and his hat, and left me to clean up. Sid's lack of an answer, even when I mentioned his beloved granddaughter, had left me convinced: he had no interest in finishing the Vincati. And without him, I didn't have a chance.

Despite Sid's black mood, a day or two later I got him to push on with Denny's Shadow. After all, that was a paying job. We put the heads and cylinders on and then finished off the rest of the motor. After that I transferred the motor from the engine bench to our air lift. Then we began to build up the bike around the motor. I was looking forward to securing the swingarm. I had studied this arrangement for so long on the Vincati that I couldn't wait to do it on a standard Vincent.

Soon Sid announced that it was quitting time. He went back into the house while I stayed to clean up and turn off all the lights.

Alone, now, an idea came to me. I went over to the Vincati, put the tank and seat on, and reattached the side covers. Then I rooted around and found its carbs, Amal Mk 1s, set up with all of Sid's favorite tricks. Holding them in my hands, they felt simple and solid. But their innards betrayed that impression. Inside those gray canisters lived a complex system of tunnels, drillings, and passages designed to blend and supply gas and air to the motor. Certain passages Sid opened up. Elsewhere he added slots and steps, either to increase fuel flow or to encourage the gas droplets to shake free from the wall. Run regularly, such mods behave beautifully. But if left to sit, such carbs are prone to gumming up. That's why he had sold the Duke. As he stopped riding her regularly, he found himself cleaning the carbs again and again. I slid the Vincati's pair onto their inlet stubs.

It was all just for show of course—we still had plenty of work to do—but the next day, when Sid opened the door, what he saw was the Vincati in its final form.

"Oh!" Sid said. Then he sat on his stool and studied it. I could see him struggling. He looked dumbstruck.

"It's beautiful, isn't it?" I said quietly, fearing that beauty now wouldn't be enough.

"Yeah," Sid said. "Lex will just love seeing this." Before Sid's accident, he had been supplying Lex with regular updates and at times he would pass me the phone.

"You owe him a call," I said. "Tell him where we are in the project.

Final mock-up. Big step. But I have a question for you? Do you think that we should run the cowl?"

The cowl shrouds the magneto and its addition changes the look of the motor, and thus of the whole bike, dramatically. I had stopped there on purpose.

"Sure. Put it on."

I secured it to the engine.

I turned and looked at Sid. "You like?"

Now a smile spread across his face. "Yes! It fills the barn door even more!" There was some life behind the words. "I see exactly what Irving had in mind when he drew the cowl. And I love how it works with the Duke's massive front forks. The two together make for quite a pair."

"So it stays?"

"Absolutely. I can't wait to see how it looks out on the road."

My plan had worked. The old passion was back:

"Rapture," Sid later called the feeling he had that day. It was an apt word for our experience with the Vincati.

That night Sid called Stan and brought him up-to-date. Then he called Lex. He tried him several times without luck. Eventually, Jeff answered.

Standing there, listening to Sid's conversation, I learned the bad news: Lex had died the previous afternoon.

While waiting for Sid to pass me the phone, I thought of everything Jeff had done for his dad and everything Lex had done for us.

Sid and I were stunned. In some ways, we'd been building this bike for Lex as much as for us. And though he'd been so sick, somehow we hadn't seen this coming. Not now. In the past every time I had talked to Lex, I had promised him that it wouldn't be too much longer and that soon I'd be telling him what the bike sounded like and how it rode. I said what I could to Jeff and he listened respectfully.

Finally, he said, "Well, next time you want to give my dad an update, you won't need to call me. Just look up when you say it."

After Sid said good-bye, we sat together quietly. I knew there'd be no more talk of quitting. I didn't say anything. I just looked at my father.

"We are going to finish this bike," Sid said.

"For Lex," I added.

Then an idea came to Sid: "And we are going to call her Polly." Polly had been Lex's wife and Jeff's mother.

One evening while we were working, I told Sid I thought we should go ahead and sell the Campbell bike.

He didn't disagree. "It sits over there like a black cloud. But why now?"

I could tell that keeping track of time was becoming more difficult for Sid so I explained it to him: three months had already passed since I got tenure. The summer was ending and we still had so much to do on the Vincati. Soon the fall would be over, too, and come January I would have to resume teaching. We needed to make this last window of time as productive as possible and that's why I had decided: it was finally time to find the Campbell Rapide that new owner he and I had always talked about.

What I couldn't say, though, was that for so long I had dreamed of the day when Sid and I would get to ride around together on our Vincents and get in that last perfect ride. Well, over the last few weeks I had come to accept that such days were permanently behind us. But I couldn't say that to Sid. Instead I told him about my other big dream: that with this extra cash in hand I would go to Martha and tell her that she should take the fall off from teaching, too. She deserved a sabbatical just as much as I did, and if the university wouldn't give her one, well then I would.

"Sounds good to me" was all Sid said. He called around and found a buyer who sent a team with a truck to collect the bike. They brought cash and asked no questions. For me the only painful aspect of the experience was watching Sid try to explain to them the minimal points of Vincent maintenance. "Where it's going," one of the men insisted, "you will never have to worry about that again. Just as long as it looks good." They didn't want a bike: they wanted a museum piece. Sid hated that.

When they left, we counted the cash.

"Go give it to Martha," Sid said. "Thirty thousand in twenties has a remarkable way of lifting one's mood."

Thus began the days of cash in the cookie jar.

With the Campbell bike gone, we were ready to roll the Vincati down onto the floor. I e-mailed my pals, looking for a buddy who would be willing to stop by and help. Bill Dean took me up on my request. He rode over on his modern Guzzi.

Bill taught biochemistry at the university, and I enjoyed riding with him. When he arrived, I had all the bikes out of the garage and on the patio. The assembly bench was positioned so that it faced the driveway.

I stood on the left and held the bars. Since we had yet to fit the front brake, I asked Bill to stand on the opposite side and hold down the rear brake manually. Sid stood on the bottom of the ramp to keep it from popping up once the bike's weight came onto it. When everyone was ready, I pushed the bike forward while Bill shoved the center stand out. The bike squealed as it slowly rolled down.

For the first time, I walked the Vincati in a circle, registering quick impressions of how the bike felt rolling. I flashed back to those Sundays riding with Sid when I took the Duke and he took the Shadow. The last time was years ago, well before I went to Duke to get my PhD.

At the time I thought there would be so many more days like that, days when Sid and I would be out riding, two men on their machines. I liked the Duke; in fact I preferred it to Sid's Shadow and he knew it. He could relax and enjoy the entire trip on his Vincent. Though we didn't know it then, we were scouting roads that I would take when I headed back down to Duke on my newly purchased Hawk.

Now I was struck by the odd connection—from Duke to Duke. And in that moment, with the Vincati before us, I realized for the first time what we we'd really been up to. We were putting the heart of the father into the body of the son.

I parked the Vincati on its side stand. Taken from an old BSA, the stand had been modified (once again by our friends the Aussies) to run on a Vincent. It was solid and confidence inspiring.

I grabbed my video camera and filmed Bill strolling over to the Vincati and then sitting on it.

"Oh yeah!" Bill laughed. "What do you think?"

"You are the first one to hop aboard. How does it feel?"

"Great."

"Work the front shocks," Sid said. "Are they too soft?"

Bill thrust the tubes down several times. "No. Solid."

He got off and Sid hobbled over. "Remove the seat," he said. I stopped filming and did as he asked. It would ensure that he could clear the bike. Bill grabbed the front forks and then Sid got on.

My dad turned to me.

"Is that on?" For a moment he was truly the old-timer who had never seen a video camera before, just a greaser on his bike.

"Yup," I said.

"Hiya, babe, how about a date?"

The old joker was hilarious.

"I'm one badass, babe!" Sid said, warming to the role. "Boy is my ass bad. So is the rest of me!"

Eventually, he stopped playacting and worked the forks some. He studied the controls then said, "This thing hurts my ass."

"Well, it needs a seat," I reminded him.

It felt good to film us all laughing. Only when I switched off the camera did I realize why I was so happy. Suddenly I was possessed again by an old desire: to write it all down.

As real fall weather settled in, Sid and I worked feverishly almost every day, alternating back and forth between the Vincati and Denny's Shadow, a project that was also in its final stages. Our garage life soon fell into a smooth, solid rhythm. I felt happy and at peace—fully aware that these were golden days. The only snags came in wiring the lights. Electronics were never Sid's strong suit, and I knew even less, but finally we got Polly's lights debugged.

As we pressed on, I noticed that Sid was beginning to struggle more and more when it came to getting up. I was worried about him.

We'd already lost so much time to his depression that I didn't want to lose the rest of my sabbatical.

"How bad is the knee?" I asked him.

"Not good," he admitted with a laugh.

"We have a good stretch left before I have to start teaching," I said. "Why don't we see if you can get a shot in the knee, and then maybe we can hold out until March and do the knee during spring break so that I'm off from school like we did before?"

"I'll try," Sid said.

My sabbatical flew by, as I feared it would. I could have gone faster to finish Polly but instead I spent as much time as I could watching Lucy grow up, and I also wanted to give Martha uninterrupted stretches to write. Ensuring that she got the time she wanted was easy to do. I didn't have to go into the university to teach, and after two or three hours out in the garage, Sid had reached his limit. That left me with lots of time to take Lucy to the zoo and to other places. Since filming Sid sitting on the Vincati, I couldn't shake this urge I felt to try to write again. I enjoyed the sensation—it was like entertaining the pleasant memory of an old girlfriend. But I didn't try to act on it. I wasn't sure I knew how to tell a story anymore—let alone this one. I wasn't that troubled though. I was having too much fun falling back in love with Martha. Those nights I fell asleep content in the knowledge that the only person in the house who needed to be writing, was.

For Sid, with a newly cortisoned knee, the pace was perfect. Alone in the garage, he communed with his bikes and slowly cleaned up the Vincati, readying it for its first start. Sid would play with the run of a cable for days, for example, looping it first like this and then like that.

First Start

Whenever I returned, I was challenged to spot and evaluate his work. The list of things he did is probably endless. I'm not sure I even know the half of it.

As the New Year approached, I decided to wait to start the bike until January 1, 2005. Fifty-five years after Sid, Johnny, and Willie made their bet about who would be the first to own a Vincent, we would start our Vincati. We toasted to good fortune shortly after midnight, and then went to bed excited to find out what we had wrought.

That first day of the year we went into the garage and looked at the Vincati. First thing to do was add our oils, a complicated ritual for Sid on a new engine. Immediate lubrication is the key to reducing wear on the parts during the first start. Sid soaked the oil filter first, before inserting it, and then pumped oil into the filter chamber and indeed every other logical entry point. The fuel system was tested next, and as I poured in gas for the first time, Sid said the only Hebrew prayer he knows, the Shema: "Hear, O Israel, the Lord our God, the Lord is One." It is considered to be the most basic declaration of faith a Jew can make and Sid never forgot it.

As for the electric starter, we had been advised to remove it and to start the bike the first time using the standard foot crank. The fear was kickback. The electric starter employs a gear that only spins in one direction, so if Polly's motor reversed direction it could snap that gear. The makers of the electric starter stressed that it was only to be used after ascertaining that the bike was indeed timed correctly and firing properly.

I wouldn't have wanted it any other way. Kick-starting was my job and with 10-to-1 compression, the Vincati would take a lot of leg. And

233

that meant much more potential for injury in the event of a kickback. Lex had 8 to 1. Sid's old Shadow had 9 to 1. Sid had built 10s before, and I had ridden at least two. If the Vincati proved to be like those, it was going to be right at the edge of my strength.

I approached the machine with great respect. I launched into the starting ritual, always a complicated sequence of little things. Adjust the choke. Tickle the carbs to ensure that you have fuel flowing into the motor. Prime the motor by working the kick start some while getting a feel for where the compression events occur in the rotation of your kick.

The Vincati's action turns out to be surprisingly swift and crisp. My foot blasts through one detonation cycle then the next, so that soon the motor taps a beat back to it—*boom boom boooom, boom boom boooom*—and you want to stop right before the lone long *boooom*. That position gives you the best shot to start a Vincent.

I gave Polly a good boot, and the motor fired perhaps five times, almost caught, and then quit.

I kicked again. This time the bike started up but quit before being able to settle into an idle.

Sid cursed.

I tried again, this time using more throttle to ensure that the bike went off, even if I had to race it. *Whooom!*

The Vincati was alive!

And the exhaust sounded wicked as hell.

I thought I was revving it pretty good, but then Sid took the throttle and really racked it open. The bike, even on its center stand, felt such motion from its spinning crankshaft that it slid backward across the floor, showing real power. I opened the garage doors while Sid revved it some more and then hit the kill button.

He put his arm around me, satisfied. As our ears adjusted to silence after that roar, he announced that the tach wasn't working and the ammeter didn't appear to be reading.

"She is also pissing oil," I said. I fell to my knees and started to peer into her guts.

So there were problems, but they were nothing compared to the thrilling sounds we had just heard.

"She's gonna be fast," Sid said.

I couldn't wait to find out.

Chapter Sixteen

Sid's Gift

For the remainder of that session and into the next, Sid tried but could not get Polly to settle down to an idle. Initially, it didn't bother him, because when he got on the throttle, the rear cylinder came in and she sounded loaded for bear. So from that he assumed we had some minor problem with the carburetion on that back jug, something easily fixable. Now he was back in his element, the master tuner on the trail of a problem.

To figure out why the rear cylinder kept cutting out, we started by checking for the obvious: an air leak. An internal combustion motor requires delivery of its fuel mixture via an intake passage that must be perfectly sealed. If there's a fissure, or a "vacuum leak," additional air invades the system and disrupts the proper mixture. The result, especially at idle or low speeds, is dilution to the point where there is insufficient gas for the motor to fire properly, if at all.

The initial test to determine if we had such an air leak was for Sid to take a can of WD-40 and spray around the carburetor and manifold while I held the throttle open to keep the bike running. If the

WD-40 invaded the motor, the firing would grow erratic, showing that there was a leak. Sure enough, the engine stumbled and then re-covered: a sure sign.

When we subsequently looked at the manifold, we spotted a crack right at the end of the piece, the result of my careless work with a wrench while tightening the nuts. We were grateful the problem was so simple to solve: a little epoxy tastefully applied and things would be good as new. But after restarting, we learned that we were wrong: the leak wasn't fixed, or if it was, then we had another, bigger problem.

Now it was my turn. I argued that we simply missed a crack, that there was another leak. We tore into the engine again and had a look. We filled the manifold with water, but there was no leak. In frustra-tion, we installed a different manifold; we reassembled and restarted and the rear cylinder still cut out. Polly had humbled both of us.

It was the dead of a cold winter, and that made it tough for Sid to move around, especially in our Spartan garage. I would take Sid to physical therapy, wait till he was done, bring him home, and then head off to teach. On my off days we worked on Polly. But that Febru-ary Sid worked every day, still trying to sort out the problem. He'd worked on hundreds of Vincent motors and he had never seen any-thing like this. We'd already jumped through so many hoops to get the Vincati on the ground, and now we were being bested by some simple tuning problem. It was almost too much for Sid to take.

One day, when I returned from class on my Hawk, I raised the ga-rage door to find Sid sitting on his stool staring at the Vincati, like a boxer trying to size up an especially dangerous opponent. It was forty degrees, the lights were out, and his coffee had gone cold. I had no idea how long he had been out there, and neither did he.

I took my helmet off and rolled in my bike. Sid looked distraught. He asked me to start the Vincati because he had a new idea of what the problem might be.

His current suspicion centered on an electrical fault, perhaps a weak condenser. A condenser acts as a reservoir, briefly building up electrical energy or "pressure," then releasing it in pulses, thereby enhancing, or "stepping up," the spark produced by the ignition system. But Sid's theory made no sense: there was only one condenser and it fired both cylinders, so why would it strike only the rear?

"I don't know!" he snapped in anger. "Just start the damn bike."

I kicked it to life. And again the ritual began. I walked around the Vincati, removing one spark-plug cap, then the other. I loaded the engine by revving the throttle. I got out the strobe light. Resembling a toy space gun with a cord that ends in a clip, the strobe flashes in concert with the spark plug to which it is clamped. I attached it to the suspect ignition wire running to the back cylinder, and we watched it flash regularly, indicating that nothing was amiss.

Sid gave up and hit the kill button. "Let's change the condenser."

And we did, even though neither of us really thought that was the problem. Sure enough, it wasn't.

The next day I found Sid sitting out there again, and when I asked if he had an idea, he just shook his head. "Just help me off of this damn stool," he said, and we walked into the house together in silence.

This nightmare stretched on and on, swallowing one day after the next. When I was not teaching, we went out together and continued to poke around the Vincati. Finally, Sid told me what he thought, and it was his worst fear.

"I think the head is damaged. The Crew, when he ported the head, he broke through the inlet wall."

As much as I had learned about Vincents, I still didn't have a clear idea of what Sid was talking about.

Sid said, "You may think the interior of a cylinder head is a simple space. You'd be wrong. It is as complex as the interior of some dark undersea set of caves. Each head has four main tunnels, and at points they come extremely close to one another. One of the tricks to making a motor go fast is to enlarge the intake, the tunnel through which the fuel mixture travels; that's what guys call 'porting.' You can get into trouble though if you open out too far and break through the wall dividing the intake tunnel from the rocker tunnel within which the oil circulates. Do that, and then oil gets sucked into your fuel mixture and fouls the plugs, with the result that the cylinder stops firing, especially at idle."

"And if that is the problem?" I asked.

Sid said, "We'd have to start over. Drop out the motor, take off the head, and seal the fissure—have a welder Heliarc it."

"No! The Crew would have spotted that."

"We all make mistakes. He's getting old. He's only a few years younger than me. None of us should be doing this anymore. It's a young man's game. I should have my head examined."

"Did you ask him?"

Sid looked at me with incredulity.

"How do you ask a man if he made a mistake like that?"

"Ask him," I insisted. "Come on, let's go in and call him."

Sid's Gift

Inside, Sid handed me the phone. The Crew is a man of incredible skills but great modesty. He rivals Sid when it comes to complaining about being old and not up to snuff anymore. Plus he has worked long enough with metal to see it do spooky things. When I asked him if there could be a crack, he said one word.

"Sure."

"If we look, can we spot it?"

"You might" was all he would venture.

After I hung up the phone, Sid and I began to digest this possibility. We were days away from surgery. Things were getting better with Martha. The Vincati project could not drag on another year. It had already swallowed five.

A sickening feeling in my stomach told me that this was the end. It ran, at least on the stand. It was pretty. Some collector would be happy to pay a lot of money just to look at it. So day after day I left to go teach, convinced that that was the story. The only question was when I would sell what was inside that garage.

But at the same time, I couldn't accept defeat. Like Sid, I felt we had to solve this problem. There was time. We had a week. If I was going to be getting that head fixed, I wanted to hold it in my hands as soon as possible.

At the next work session, we removed the rear carburetor and its manifold. Now we had direct access to the inlet channel that flows through the cylinder head and stops at the intake valve. When the intake valve is depressed, it provides entrance into the combustion chamber and the piston. Armed with a selection of dental equipment—probes, picks, mirrors, and tiny lights—we looked for a fissure, hoping to find the crack without removing the cylinder head. Sid was standing behind me with a light, and I started painstakingly running over the inner walls with a dental probe, feeling for a crack.

"What's that glint?" Sid asked.

"Where?"

"On the valve. It's fresh oil, isn't it?"

I looked. "Yeah."

"If there's oil in there, it must be cracked," Sid said. "How else could it get there?"

My heart sank. I put the probe down and looked at him. "Do you want to go ahead and start dropping out the motor?"

He had tears in his eyes. It took everything he had just to get up. The stress he was putting on his shoulders was destroying what remained of his rotor cuffs. He could barely click off a light switch. And for what? A museum piece that won't even run?

"Help me up," Sid said, finally. He looked inconsolable.

I stood alongside his stool, with one hand under his arm and the other ready to hoist him by his belt.

He rocked back and forth slightly. "One, two, three!" he said and then tried to stand.

But we didn't get a good enough launch, and he collapsed back onto the stool. While he gathered his strength for a second attempt, we looked at the Vincati. It sat about two feet in the air, secured on our lift.

"It looks like a patient on a gurney," Sid said with a laugh.

"Well, doctor," I said, "it's up to us to fix it."

"What if I can't? I feel like it's got us whipped."

"We'll figure it out," I said.

"I sure hope I'm better after this operation," Sid said.

"You better be. I can't do this alone."

Sid readied himself for another attempt at rising. "One, two, three, lift!"

This time I really put my weight into it, and he stood. Once again I felt my hands tingle. Eventually, I would end up going to Makk for cortisone shots to combat the inflammation, but right then I didn't care. We walked toward the garage door.

"We got to figure this problem out now," Sid said. "Just look at it. Dead on the lift." A moment later he added, "That could be me in a few days."

"We will figure it out," I said firmly. "But that may not happen till you come back from the hospital."

"Well, this time I may not come back."

I looked at him.

"Matthew, I can't help it. I can't stop thinking about it, and if that is what is on my mind when they put me out, I'm afraid I may not come back."

In his eyes I saw real fear mixed with utter conviction.

The next day we went back out. I sensed that Sid wanted me to take the motor out. But after sleeping on it, I refused to believe that the problem was a cracked head. I knew the Crew. He wouldn't have, couldn't have, made this mistake. It had to be something else, anything else.

"There is nothing else," Sid insisted. "Just drop the goddamn motor." He moved over to our workbench and started another task. He couldn't even bear to watch.

I started the air compressor and then raised the lift to its full extension to get the Vincati's motor at eye level, where I need it to do the job.

"You saw the oil," Sid said, while fiddling with a set of spring boxes bound for a customer's Shadow.

"What if it got there another way?"

Sid let out a pained laugh.

"Well, the rings haven't seated," I said. "Fresh oil blowing by the rings, especially once the plug in the rear cylinder fouls and it's running on just the front jug."

As the Brits said long ago, oil is devilish stuff, and extremely tricky to control. Motors require a minimal "oil film," just sufficient to control wear and prevent seizure between each individual piston and the round cylinder liner in which it lives. To ensure that this happens, the engine's lubricating oil must not be allowed to migrate from beneath the piston's "skirt," where it does its job, to above the piston, where combustion occurs. The barrier is the piston's rings. Riding in grooves or "ring lands," the piston's rings extend out a few thousandths of an inch and once properly broken in, or "burnished," they serve as seals, allowing past only that needed trace of oil.

We had not run the Vincati enough to break it in, so we were still seeing white smoke out of the exhaust, a sign that the rings had not seated, and so we were getting far too much oil above the piston. I was imagining a scenario in which oil got sucked up in sufficient quantity for it to seep beyond the intake valve, thus explaining the small puddle we found in the intake passageway.

Sid put his wrench down and looked at me. He knew my explanation was possible. Now he had no idea what to do. I was seeing him in a moment of absolute failure. But I wasn't angry; I just felt sorry for him.

"Do you want me to continue?" I said.

"How the hell should I know? I don't know anything anymore. We need to think about this before we undo five years of work. Help me up."

The mood was unbearable. After Sid was settled in his recliner, I decided to do the one thing that would make me feel better. I headed toward the door.

"Going for a ride?" Sid asked glumly.

"Gotta clear my head."

On Lex, I headed out Brownsboro Road to an old, rarely used boat landing at the end of a nice twisty country lane. I often go there to pace the parking lot and think. While looking at the sunset over the Ohio River, I got an idea. Sid was so consumed with beating himself up over his inability to find the problem that he had gotten away from basics.

At the next session, I insisted we start fresh. I led Sid to where he sits on his stool next to the Vincati. As I was about to start the bike I said, "Just listen to the motor and tell me what you hear."

I started the Vincati and then held a towel over the exhaust pipe to muffle it. For a minute the two of us sat there, and the only sound in the garage was the whirring of the motor—all those interrelated movements, hundreds of pieces in motion. Sid peered intently, as if he were Superman and could look through the motor's cases. Then he whispered in a voice that was half-stunned, "If I wasn't going crazy, I'd swear the rear cam has slipped."

Now I may not have believed Sid when he told me about seeing ghosts after his heart attack, but when it comes to engine sounds, I trust him with my life.

I stopped the bike, and off came the pipes and the timing chest cover and the steady plate and the push rods, and I handed him the rear cam.

In a motor, cams control when the valves open and shut. They consist of a shaft carrying at least one oval metal eccentric or "lobe." The cam on this machine has two. Finally, a gear is driven onto one end of the camshaft in a "press fit." The result is a mating of the two pieces so that the camshaft turns with this gear rather than spinning freely within it. We located a spare cam and placed it end to end with the Vincati's rear cam and discovered that the lobes did not align. Just as Sid had divined, the Vincati's rear camshaft was slipping within its gear.

So it wasn't a cracked head, and we weren't dead in the water.

We had caught the problem, and just in time. If this movement had continued, the piston and the valves would have grown so far out of sync that they would have collided, causing catastrophic damage. As for the cause, a demon had crept in through a tiny flaw: an absent shim in the timing chest. The resulting drag was enough to break the camshaft free from its gear's grip. The fault must have occurred when Sid took those first big twists of the throttle right after we brought the bike to life.

Despite his recent laments about being "finished," this was the most incredible display of Sid's craft I had ever seen. I can't begin to imagine what he heard in those sounds. I couldn't hear anything different. But Sid had. When I asked him about it later, Sid said that he could hear through the carburetors that the rear cylinder's intake valve was closing an instant behind the front's and introducing a delayed *sh-thunk* into the motor's regular percussive rhythm.

Sid's Gift

With no time to waste, Sid went back into the house to call John Healy. John owned Coventry Spares, a business specializing in parts for vintage British bikes. He and Sid had been doing business for decades.

By the time I caught up to Sid, he was holding his hand over the phone.

"He says he has a set right on the shelf. They're rare—Black Lightning racing cams made by Andrews. Five hundred dollars for the pair. They were in Rip Tragle's old stock." Rip was another master Vincent builder back in the day.

Sid was expecting me to blanch at the cost. I didn't blink. "Have them sent overnight."

The Andrews cams arrived the next day, and by that same afternoon the bike was ready. I booted the Vincati to life, this time hearing at once the healthy *ba-boom, ba-boom* of both cylinders firing in a nice even idle. Sid, of course, heard more. He reached for his pocket screwdriver and wrench and began to circle the bike, fettling. He let in a little more air in one cylinder, lowered the slide on the other.

I watched, as always, in amazement at this gift.

I saw serenity in my dad as he worked doing what he loved best—fettling. He didn't need any machines, just his own intuition.

Sid caught my eye. "Go ride her."

"Now?"

"Hell yes."

I killed the motor and while the bike sat, its engine making a regular metallic tinking sound, I quickly opened the garage door, made a path, and suited up. I left the helmet in the garage, though. I needed to be able to hear the motor on this first run.

I kicked and Polly roared awake. As I rocked her off the center stand, I listened to her peculiar loping chuckle. I studied the acrid smell of the exhaust for any odd or new scents.

It was immediately clear that Polly didn't like to idle, no race bike does—they want to go. You have to develop a sense for blipping the throttle to prevent a stall, just enough to avoid racing the motor. With a quick wave at Sid, I engaged bottom gear with an easy lift of the foot, released the clutch on a rising throttle, and in an instant the bike rolled down the driveway under its own power.

With my heart pounding, I turned out into the street, still feathering the clutch. I was terrified and excited at once. It's easy to drop a bike on the first ride. What if the brakes failed? What if there was a spot of oil on the new unscuffed tires and I went down at the first corner, right where Sid last fell?

More than anything, I felt intense pressure to pull off this first ride. I rounded the corner fine and then hit the throttle, and in a flash I could tell that the Vincati revved so damn fast that it had no use for bottom gear. On a Vincent, anything faster than a walking speed in first feels unpleasant. Normally, I am in second by the time the bike hits 15 mph, but on the Vincati I made my first shift at around 35 mph. I was basically taxiing to the first long stretch in our neighborhood, a cross street that runs about three city blocks.

As I trundled along, I settled into the seat and discovered that I still loved the way a Ducati chassis from the seventies sits: long and relaxed, perfectly suited for a big twin motor, offering classic ergodynamics.

Now I had some road ahead and I rolled it on in second, and in the next instant the bike entered its power band, literally rising on its haunches and loading the back wheel, further increasing its surge. I glanced down at the speedo and saw 75 mph, and I was still in second with the throttle barely cracked, about two blocks past my garage. Only then did the Vincati truly begin to charge hard, passing 85 mph, at which point I sensed that I could easily hoist its front wheel.

And there were still two more gears.

I realized then that I couldn't just ride around the neighborhood and return to Sid with a solid rider's report.

Tuning, like life, is a series of compromises. Long-legged bikes have their power band shifted to the top end, while torque monsters, bikes with grunt, give it to you from the get-go. In keeping with Irving's design philosophy, a standard Vincent features a smartly chosen compromise that seeks to offer the rider the fun that comes when the bike can do both. But not the Vincati, at least not in that first state of tune: it was all top end. Sid had wished for a bike that could streak across the salt, and the Crew had given him what he wanted.

I circled back to the house. Sid's face was pale and his brow was furrowed. He thought something was wrong.

"Back so soon?"

"I need my helmet."

"Why?"

"I've got to take it out on the road. I can't get it out of second gear if I stay in the development. For it to pull at all in third, I have to be going well over a 100 mph."

Sid was shocked. With the exception of first, Vincents normally have very elastic gearing. Whether in second, third, or top, Irving's transmission usually allows the rider to remain in the gear selected over a wide range of speed. This characteristic is especially true of third. Normally, I shift into third well before hitting 30 mph.

I could tell I would have to be forceful for him to accept what I was saying. "I have to keep the revs up or it starts knocking. By the tach, anything below about 2,500 rpm and it's not happy."

"Yeah." Sid nodded.

"Well, 2,500 rpm in second is 85 mph. To shift into third and stay there I need to be going 100 mph."

Again Sid was stunned. "It's those cams."

Before we had put them in, we had compared them with our original factory cams and they were radically different.

"Is it strong?" he asked.

"I can't tell yet."

Sid circled the bike to make sure everything was good and then he handed me my helmet, saying, "Do what you got to do."

I knew what Sid meant. I had to take her to a favorite stretch out in the country where I felt comfortable really getting on the throttle. If we were going to learn how it behaved in third or fourth at speed, I had to be willing to take some risks.

Sid didn't just want to know that it can putt along in third. He wanted me to tell him how the bike behaved when you get into the meat of the torque curve, which on a Vincent happens around 4,000 rpm. If I was right, that meant visiting the dangerous end of the dial.

Normally, I don't like to ride far out into the country on a brand-new bike, but on this day I had no choice. I got Martha's cell phone and handed it to Sid. Then I put my helmet on, started the bike, and pulled away.

I headed out to a road I know that runs to Goshen. It's a stretch I like, a straight two-lane country road without cross traffic as it cuts through a bowl in the farmland. In second, I cruised along at about 70, carefully looking for any farm equipment; then when I came to the rise, I slowed to a walk and turned the bike around.

It's best to do these things fast. When it comes to speed, space is precious and I wanted to use every bit of road in order to launch the bike.

The moment I was straight again, I hit the throttle and shifted into second. This time when I approached 85 mph I shifted again, and as third came in I rolled on more and the bike responded instantly, lifting up and charging. My eyes flicked over to the speedo, where I saw the needle moving above 100 mph. After a moment of rush, I shifted again and the bike settled into a pleasant cruise in fourth, around 110 mph. Then I gave it a little more gas and the Vincati responded immediately, coming onto the cam in a sudden rush. During peak performance, the pulses of air entering through the carburetors arrive in sync with the opening and closing of the engine's valves. The result is optimal use of each cylinder's volume for the creation of power. For me the sensation is reminiscent of rowing a boat. When all the oars work together, you can feel the boat rise and fall as it "walks" through the water. Similarly, with each detonation the Vincati hurtled through space, and I sensed that it wanted nothing but more road and time to go even faster. Then just as quickly, I bottomed out and the road began to rise. While climbing up the other side, I scrubbed off speed as I shifted back into third and then second.

The surge was unbelievable. I have never experienced anything like it on another Vincent—not Lex, nor Denny's newly resurrected Shadow, both of which are joys to ride but neither could come close to Polly. Sure, any top-drawer modern sport bike like the SV could do it. But Polly was special: heavy and gangly and, as it is a V-twin, it feels much like a modern Guzzi. Yet it is fifty years older than that, and its sounds, to me, are old friends. Its smells, feel, gait—all stirred power-fully new emotions in me, and yet old emotions, too.

As I blasted down the road, a picture formed in my mind of a young, healthy Sid: that uniformed Yank visiting the Vincent works and vowing to Mr. Vincent that he would do him proud.

Well, with this bike Sid had made good on that promise. In fact he had accomplished his goal almost too well. In that state of tune, Polly was perfect for a speed run at Bonneville. But that wasn't the real world. That was the world of Sid's dreams.

When I got back to the house, I told Sid we would have to make some adjustments. Because Polly was alive, and there was a world out there, with roads to ride—and there was Lucy. After all it was her bike.

Sid understood, or said he did. We put on a fifty-tooth rear sprocket (forty-six is standard for a Vincent). This simple swap raised the rpm and gave it more of a usable lower end. With that change, I could actually use second as an in-town gear. We also went in on the carbu-retors' air screws and richened up the mixture, a change that robs the bike of acceleration but helps ensure that you don't burn up pistons.

With those adjustments, I took Polly out again, and this time she truly stole my heart. With this combination, not only did I have a hot Vincent motor, but thanks to the Duke chassis I had better brakes and suspension and an entirely different steering feel. A Vincent is top-heavy: you muscle it through corners, dropping the bars; the Vincati, however, is a bike you steer with your ass. It is very comfortable and smooth. You feel like you are settled into a nice couch, when in real-ity you're flying down the road.

Sid's Gift

After putting about fifty miles on her that second time out, I started to relax. I imagined myself with Lucy on the back and a mess of camping gear stashed in saddlebags. Hell, maybe even with a side-car. Martha always said she would go for that. Riding along I decided: Polly was much better than a standard Vincent or any other Vincent-powered special I had ever ridden. Better, too, than the silver Duke.

Perfect, in fact.

Or at least that is how it felt rifling along a narrow road, between stands of towering trees. I listened to my breath under the constant thrumming of the exhaust. The bike had slowed, as had my heart.

I thrust my head forward into the blue-smeared sky and rode.

Chapter Seventeen

Strange Beach

By September 2005, Sid was far enough along in his recovery from the second knee surgery that I began to think it might be possible to give him one last gift. So I canceled a week's worth of classes and surprised him with two tickets to Salt Lake City. From there we rented a car and got on I-80 headed west. As we approached Utah's border with Nevada, we saw the sign I had told Sid to keep an eye out for: BONNEVILLE RACECOURSE.

The occasion was the second-annual BUB Motorcycle Speed Trials. Of course I wished we had taken the Vincati, but I didn't have the money. I hesitated about going at all. Somehow it seemed wrong—hollow—to go without a bike. Then one evening, Martha pulled me aside, just as she has so many times before when it mattered, and said, "Can't you see, he just wants to go? Take him, for God's sake."

Once we arrived on the salt, I slowed the car to an idle and nudged along the far edge of the pits, looking for the Vincent contingent. After we passed a few racers, we hit pay dirt: there was our dear buddy

Max Lambky, who was with his twin-engine Vincent Streamliner and next to him was pitted Steve Hamel with his Vincent special.

After I brought the car to a halt, I hopped out and circled around to help Sid. Before he stood up, Sid reached down and pressed a finger to the ground and then licked it. "Yep, that's salt," he said.

Once up, Sid turned slowly, taking in the scene. Around us the white salt blazed like we were standing on an unbroken mirror. In the distance gnarled dusky mountains hovered on the horizon.

"Lex, old buddy," Sid said, "we're here."

Once inside the Lambky tent, we found more old friends, including Marty Dickerson, who had burst onto the scene long ago. Back when Rollie Free got his own Lightning and upped the American class-A record to a speed of 156.58, along came Marty who, in 1950, had rode his stock Rapide to a new class-C (for pump gas, as opposed to A for alcohol) record of 141.72. Sid had not seen Marty since the rally in Boone, North Carolina, back in 1996 when I met G, the man who sourced me the Vincati chassis.

Hearing of Sid's arrival, Denis Manning (the Big Ugly Bastard behind BUB) showed Sid around his record breaker. Though sidelined then with computer problems, Manning's BUB liner would soon record a speed of 350.88 mph and become the world's fastest motorcycle. They talked of the Vincent factory where Denis had gotten his start before striking it big in the aftermarket-parts biz. Sid told Denis that he still used an old trick of his—pouring a can of classic Coke down the muffler to sweeten the exhaust note.

While they chatted, I walked over to see how Steve Hamel was doing. I hadn't seen him since Mid-Ohio in 1998, when I had ridden my Hawk up to Vintage Days. He was fielding, for just the second year, a standard Vincent that he had modified with exquisite care. He was on a personal quest to top Rollie's 150.313. I wished him luck and then led Sid back over to the Lambky tent.

I asked Marty, "What's the fastest you ever saw on that Rapide of yours?"

"A hundred and forty-seven miles per hour on the public highway outside of LA."

After a while I called Martha and told her again how much I loved her. She was right—I needed to take Sid to Bonneville, even if all we could do was watch. Eventually, a different voice came on the line.

"Are you at the salt beach?" Lucy asked.

"I sure am, honey bunny!"

"But there is no swimming?"

"It's a strange beach, Lucy."

"You and Pop Pop have fun with all your junk!"

As I laughed, I heard Steve fire up his Vincent. Sid and I followed him up to the start. Later his wife, Wendy, proudly held up the slip: 153 mph.

As another bike began its run, my dad looked over at me and said, "I wish I could have ridden the Vincati just once."

Then from a loud speaker, the announcer interrupted: "He's just entering the timed section now."

We listened to the racer's wail as it rose in pitch, peaked, and then faded away.

"But that's okay," Sid added. "All these Vincents, the ones still on the road, they're my babies. Tuning them is why God put me on earth."

BIG SID'S VINCATI

* * *

Late the next afternoon, we were all waiting for the Lambky liner to do a return run when the word went out that the racetrack was shutting down. The water was rising in the lake: the course would soon get flooded, and the winds were kicking up. The rest of the meet was scrubbed.

Now unexpectedly, Big Sid and I had two days to kill. With nothing better to do, I bought some maps. While Sid nursed a cup of coffee, I sat at a picnic table at a rest stop and studied the roads with the aim of picking a destination. As I read the colorful names of small towns and noted nearby scenic routes, I felt again that urge to tell a good story. Soon I was back behind the wheel, driving toward the sea and listening to Sid talk about the Whizzer he once owned and how sometimes at night he could still hear the sharp note of its exhaust. As we approached a small town called Garden City, on the shore of Bear Lake, I slid the windows down and the mountain air filled the car. Sid took a deep breath and closed his eyes.

After a while he said, "Of all the bikes I've ever worked on, the Vincati is the best thing I ever did."

I looked over at him. I understood, because I want to live to be his age and say that about the last thing I write.

Epilogue: Every Day

Not long after that trip, *Cycle World* sent its best-loved writer, Peter Egan, to ride the Vincati. I'll always treasure the look on the photographer's face when I sheepishly admitted to him that Sid and I had never gotten around to buying a trailer. Polly did a hundred trouble-free miles that day, and Peter's piece is a real gem. The bike got the centerfold, and even the Midnight Crew smiled when I gave him a signed copy.

By then Sid and I had started a new project: a Vincent single, finished in trim proper for running at Bonneville (after all, I promised Lex the chassis wouldn't go to waste). Steve Hamel is doing us a favor and punching the motor out from 500 to 600 cc. A specially made modern piston just arrived for it, and I picked up the seat last weekend. It matches the one we did for the Vincati. And the base is from the old seat I took off Sid's Shadow before we sold it. I tell guys that somebody has to field a Vincent single at the BUB meet. It's another quest to keep Sid going.

Epilogue: Every Day

We have also taken on more restoration work. The next big, paying job turned out to be the full rebuild of a motor from out of another "Chinese Red" Rapide. If Sid hasn't worked on every single one from that batch, he has come close. At first Sid said no, claiming that he was too old and starting to forget things. It's true—he can't tell you his own phone number or our street address. But generally he is doing well. He has his aches and pains, but we go out to the garage almost every day, and though he wishes he could ride, he loves to be among his bikes and to hear me talk about riding, something I can't help but do. And despite his forgetfulness—the difference between Amal Mk 1s and 2s, mags and distributors, Rapide and Shadow cams, and a thousand other things—for now, they're still on the tip of his tongue.

With each new customer I say, Sid is getting too old and this is going to be our last big one. At this point guys just laugh, because Sid's still sharp despite his age. Bob Bailey was here from Maryland last weekend to drop off his pretty Rapide. After Bob left, Sid turned to me and said, "If they say it has been sitting for three years, think six."

Despite my doubts about what motorcycles have done to me, I can't let them go. I fall asleep hearing exhaust. One afternoon I returned from a ride on Lex. I had gotten caught in a rain shower. I took off my riding gear and started to wipe her down. The bike was still hot and radiating a strong smell. Sid was sitting at the bench, working, and started talking about recognizing your bike by its smell. It's not just gas and oil; it's the road grime, all the places you've moved through—this is the real reason grizzled old guys don't like to clean their bikes. At that I stopped and looked at the dirty rags in my hands and fought back tears.

Epilogue: Every Day

For better or worse, I pass this love on. Not too long ago, I gave Lucy her first ride on a Vincent. We putted around while neighbors stopped their yard work to watch, and Lucy released one hand from my belt to wave. No fear, that girl.

Now she too wants to ride every day.

Notes

The Vincatis

As of 2008, seven Vincatis have been built. The builders are Max Johnson, Don Henderson, Ian Brock, Neal Videan (who built his using an SS chassis), Phil Pilgrim, Bruce Armfield (who fitted a sidecar), and Big Sid. Except for Big Sid, all are Australian. The photo I brought to the hospital that night was of Armfield's Vincati.

Polly's Specs

The power unit began life in basic Rapide tune with 6.45-to-1 compression and inlet manifolds 1¹⁄₁₆ inches in diameter. We punched that out to 10-to-1 compression with 32 mm inlets fed by Amal concentric Mk 1s. The intake ports have been enlarged to match. The exhaust ports are massaged to increase discharge area. The roof is raised and the passageway widened on either side of the guide so that it tapers out toward the exhaust pipe flange. The lower guides are made from Ampco-wrought bronze and carry a Viton seal. The pistons are NOS (new old stock) Specialloid racing pieces (as were used in the factory Black Lightnings) and have been trimmed down from 10.5 to 1 to lessen the possibility of detonation. The area around the inlet valves has been reshaped to facilitate flow.

Fresh 60 thou oversized liners create good thermal paths, aided by blueprinted muffs, thus ensuring parallel surfaces. Their bottoms are sealed by O-rings that ride in a groove turned in the underside of the muff at the edge of the liner. We also lightened the flywheels, cutting them on a slant across the rims toward their outer faces. A pound and a quarter of steel was removed, thus reducing inertia and facilitating quick revving. The big end is a late Alpha with silver-plated INA racing cages. The main shafts have tougher metal pins (replacing the Mills pins) and are locked against movement with bearing rollers driven into drillings then peened over and polished. These steps are done to prevent shifting of the mainshafts during violent launches and are located on the inner face of the wheels, half in the wheel and half in the shaft.

The left-side mains carry a double-lipped seal between the bearing assemblies, this to prevent the passage of air or oil to and from the primary chain case. Two passages in the inner crankcase wall are enlarged by a quarter inch to facilitate the evacuation of sump pressure into the timing chest. Oil is supplied to the ball race in the outer primary through a cupped drilling where it wets the seal and flows back through the balls. A double-speed oil-pump worm is used (an original Picador piece supplied by Ken Tidswell), hard-chromed followers (supplied by Colin Taylor), and a Lightning steel big idler gear.

Notes

We have replaced the Andrews cams with the original Mk 2 Lightning cams after they were repaired. It is now running a twenty-two-tooth Black Lightning countershaft sprocket and a fifty-tooth rear. The results yield a substantial gain in low-end power at the expense of some top-end surge, but we judge the trade worth it. Additional tailoring of the ignition advance curve improved idling and acceleration. The result produces an estimated 80 bhp with a top speed of about 150 mph.

We use a modern multiplate wet clutch (supplied by Neal Videan), and the primary sports Videan's kit, consisting of an ESA (engine shock absorber) with a doubled quantity of springs and rubber-covered tensioner blade. Ignition is handled by a modern 12-volt coil run off a Lucas D distributor (with a modern condenser) driven by a plastic gear. On the Lucas, the driveshaft carries a pair of Viton O-rings and the advance weight plate is brazed in place. A modern alternator and an electric starter, both French built, round out a full 12-volt system that feeds halogen lights.

Handling is much improved with thirteen-inch (from eye to eye) Koni dampers. Because Ducati and Vincent engines weigh roughly the same, little frame overload is manifest; however, half-inch preload spacers above the front fork springs were fitted.

Initial recommended setting for the Amal Mk 1s: 260/270 main jet (to suit the Australian-made straight-through silencer), 106 needle jet, #3 slide, needle in middle notch, idle mixture screw 1¼ turns out. Slide height to start 1⅛ turn up from the edge, just breaking.

Spark-plug gap is 30 to 32 thou; distributor point gap is 12 thou. Ignition timing fully advanced thirty-five degrees BTDC with idle right at TDC. We have had excellent results with ND plugs W22EPU.

With the rider's weight on the saddle, ½ to 1 inch free play in the rear chain; with the motor hot, the primary chain should have ⅜ to ½ inch slack.

Oil recommendations (after seating rings): Valvoline 20/50 racing in the oil tank; one quart 85/90 wt hypoid in the gearbox, and the wet multiplate clutch runs in Mobil 1 ATF. For tire pressure, Matthew prefers 26 to 28 psi front and 30 to 32 rear.

Acknowledgments

From Big Sid: I am deeply grateful to the friends who rode with me. Some made it into my son's book but many more, sadly, did not. All, however, blessed my life. Some names: Ronnie Barrale, Bill Jean, Benny Doughtrey, Bill Hoddinott, Stan Ellefson, Tommy McDermott, Bugs, Mac, Ralph James, Willie Wooten, Johnny Marshall, Alex Smith, Ed Dotson, Don Henderson, Gene Aucott, John Andrews, Steve Luff, Eddie Boomhower, Somer Hooker, Steve Hamel, Ken Pettiford, Gordon Waligorski, Roland Baker, Max Lambky, Jameson Welch, Roger and Bev Weir, Boris Murray, Larry Carmack, Ray Nielson, Jim Simons, Andy Sekelsky, George Varner, Neville Higgins, and Ken Horner. Thanks go as well to our parts suppliers at the Vincent Spares Company, Maughan and Sons, June and Russell Kemp at Vin-Parts, Colin and Annie Jenner of Conways, and, most especially, John, Sue, and Tom Healy of Coventry Spares. I also want to thank Denny Cornett, Joe Walsh, Bob Bailey, and all the other motorcyclists who have entrusted me with their bikes. I especially treasure my friendship with

Acknowledgments

Phil and Edith Irving, along with so many other members of the Vincent Owner's Club. At the top of that list stands Lex—Matthew and I couldn't have done it without you. Other generous and caring backers include Kay and Bobby Reynolds, Morton Goldfarb, Keith Hazelton, Keith Cambell, and Dave Mungenast. Matthew, Martha, and Lucy Jane keep me safe, warm, and loved. And to David, Linda, and Robin—each of you holds a special place in my heart.

From Matthew: Above all—much love and thanks to my friends and family. My agent, Byrd Leavell, saw a book when no one else did, not even me. My editors, Luke Dempsey and Meghan Stevenson, made the end result incalculably better, as did the entire Hudson Street Press team. Bob Hower provided both incredible photography and invaluable friendship. Finally, I owe a great debt to Pete Fornatale for helping this English professor remember how to tell a good story.

But Lucy gets the last word: Thanks to my mom, to Bob for taking my picture, and to my dad for finally finishing this thing!